Naomi F. Zucker

YO-BZK-884

ROBERT FROST ON WRITING

ROBERT FROST
on writing

by Elaine Barry

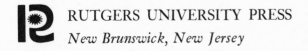
RUTGERS UNIVERSITY PRESS
New Brunswick, New Jersey

Copyright © 1973 by Rutgers University, the State University of New Jersey

Manufactured in the United States of America by Quinn & Boden Company, Inc., Rahway, New Jersey

Library of Congress Cataloging in Publication Data
Frost, Robert, 1874–1963.
　　Robert Frost on writing.

　　Bibliography: p.
　　1. Frost, Robert, 1874–1963. 2. American poetry—
20th century—History and criticism. I. Barry,
Elaine, 1937–　　II. Title.
PS3511.R94Z52　1973　　　808.1　　　73-10103
ISBN 0-8135-0692-1 Cloth
　　　 0-8135-0789-8 Paper

Grateful acknowledgment is made to Holt, Rinehart and Winston, Inc. for the reprinting of material from

Selected Letters of Robert Frost edited by Lawrance Thompson. Copyright © 1964 by Holt, Rinehart and Winston, Inc.

Letters of Robert Frost to Louis Untermeyer. Copyright © 1963 by Holt, Rinehart and Winston, Inc.

The Poetry of Robert Frost edited by Edward Connery Lathem. Copyright 1916, 1923, 1930, 1934, 1939, © 1967, 1969 by Holt, Rinehart and Winston, Inc. Copyright 1944, 1945, 1951, © 1958, 1962 by Robert Frost. Copyright © 1967, 1973 by Lesley Frost Ballantine.

Selected Prose of Robert Frost edited by Hyde Cox and Edward Connery Lathem. Copyright 1939, 1954, © 1960, 1967 by Holt, Rinehart and Winston, Inc. Copyright 1946, © 1959 by Robert Frost. Copyright © 1956 by The Estate of Robert Frost.

Conversations on the Craft of Poetry by Cleanth Brooks and Robert Penn Warren. Copyright © 1961 by Holt, Rinehart and Winston, Inc.

Grateful acknowledgment is made to The Estate of Robert Frost, Alfred C. Edwards, Executor, for permission to print here for the first time certain unpublished letters, essays and lectures. Copyright © 1973 by The Estate of Robert Frost.

"Portrait d'une Femme": Ezra Pound, *Personae.* Copyright 1926 by Ezra Pound. Reprinted by permission of New Directions Publishing Corp. Australian rights to "Portrait d'une Femme" by permission of Faber and Faber Ltd, London.

Introduction to the Arts Anthology: Dartmouth Verse, 1925. All Rights Reserved. Reprinted by permission of the Trustees of Dartmouth College, The Estate of Robert Frost and Holt, Rinehart and Winston, Inc.

Robert Frost, New American Poet, first published in the *Boston Evening Transcript* for May 8, 1915. Appears in *Interviews with Robert Frost* edited by Edward Connery Lathem. Copyright © 1966 by Holt, Rinehart and Winston, Inc.

The Introduction to *King Jasper,* by Edward Arlington Robinson, copyright © 1935, 1963, is reprinted by permission of the Macmillan Co.

Letters Nos. 53, 73, 61, 70, 123, 129, 176, 290, 302, and 57 from *Selected Letters of Robert Frost,* edited by Lawrance Thompson and Letters from PP. 165–66, 42–43, 112–114, and 246, "The Cow's on the Corn" and "John L. Sullivan Enters Heaven," from *The Letters of Robert Frost to Louis Untermeyer,* edited by Louis Untermeyer, are reprinted by permission of Jonathan Cape, Ltd.

"Robert Frost and the Sound of Sense," by Robert Newdick, *American Literature* 9:298, is reprinted by permission of Duke University Press.

Excerpts from *Robert Frost: Life and Talks-Walking,*" by Louis Mertins, © 1965, are reprinted by permission of the University of Oklahoma Press.

Passages from "Robert Frost," by Richard Poirier, in *Writers at Work: The Paris Review Interviews,* Second Series, copyright © 1963, are reprinted by permission of The Viking Press, Inc.

To the memory
of
my mother and father

Contents

Prefaces

Reviews

Lectures

Interviews

Parodies

Contents

Preface

These texts of Robert Frost's comments on writing make no pretence to comprehensiveness; with new letters and manuscript material still becoming available, the Frost canon is by no means stable enough or final enough for that. The aim has been rather to present the essence of Frost's aesthetic theories and critical judgments, while demonstrating the variety of his critical expression. Consequently, the interpretative analysis that accompanies the texts, though based on a larger body of evidence than is contained within them, offers no more than an introductory guideline to an important aspect of Frost's achievement. The focus will sharpen, and the appreciation broaden, as new evidence becomes available. But this, at least, is a start: a drawing together of statements and judgments that Frost left scattered in a multitude of writings, and a tentative analysis of the directions in which they point.

This project could not have been undertaken without the practical and generous support of the American Council of Learned Societies, which awarded me a year's Fellowship, and Monash University, which granted me leave from teaching duties. My appreciation of the help and co-operation of each is acknowledged here.

I am indebted to Mr. Alfred Edwards, trustee of the Frost estate, for permission to look at certain unpublished material; to Plymouth State College, The Library of Congress, and Stanford, Texas, Pennsylvania State, Columbia, and New York Universities for permission to photocopy and use their manuscripts under the usual copyright restrictions; to Mrs. Lesley Frost Ballantine, and to various close friends of Frost (especially Dr. Jack Hagstrom and Mr. Joseph Blumenthal) for allowing me to share the advantage of their personal knowledge of him. I owe a special debt to Professor Lawrance Thompson of Princeton University for the generous and gracious giving of his time and advice and for detailed information on many specific references.

Any appreciation of the help of Mrs. Anna May Weaver, who typed the manuscript under difficult conditions, can hardly be summarized here. Finally, I am grateful to members of the Rutgers English Department for their advice and encouragement: to Professor Richard Poirier for first suggesting the possibility of this project and to Professors Walter Bezanson and David Weimer for their help in carrying it through.

Elaine Barry

Monash University,
Melbourne, Australia

Part I
Frost as a Literary Critic

THE SCOPE OF FROST'S CRITICISM

The best critics have frequently been practicing poets—Dryden, Coleridge, Arnold, Eliot—and although the reverse is obviously not true, there is always something particularly valuable in the critical theories and judgments of a good poet. His ideas have a ring of authenticity. Since 1963, the publication of much primary material has extended our appreciation of Robert Frost and modified the myth. Most of his prose prefaces and interviews and some occasional lectures have been collected; many, not all, of his remarkable letters, suppressed during his lifetime, have been edited; the official biography is appearing. Although much remains to be done before we can have anything like a complete picture of the poet, this recent work has uncovered new facets of his mind, new dimensions of his achievement. One such dimension, particularly valuable in a poet of Frost's stature, lies in his role as a literary critic.

It should perhaps be said at the outset that Frost was not a great critic; he was hardly a conscious, let alone a conscientious one. There is not the capacity for sweeping cultural synthesis that T. S. Eliot demonstrates, little of the particularized astuteness of Ezra Pound, not the formal sense of creating a national identity through language that Yeats has. Yet Frost has more of each of these qualities than he has hitherto been credited with. Temperamentally akin to Eliot in his conservatism, Frost expresses similar views of the necessity for objectivity in art, and of the artist's interaction with the past. When Frost writes in 1954, for example,

Approach to the poem must be from afar off, even generations off. A reader should close in on it on converging lines from many directions like the divisions of an army upon a battlefield.

A poem is best read in the light of all the other poems ever written. We read A the better to read B (we have to start somewhere; we may get very little out of A). We read B the better to read C, C the better to read D, D the better to go back and

3

get something more out of A. Progress is not the aim, but circulation. The thing is to get among the poems where they hold each
other apart in their places as the stars do,[1]

he is really very close to T. S. Eliot's "Tradition and the Individual
Talent," written in 1919:

> [W]hat happens when a new work of art is created is some-
> thing that happens simultaneously to all the works of art which
> preceded it. . . . The existing order is complete before the new
> work arrives; for order to persist after the supervention of novelty,
> the *whole* existing order must be, if ever so slightly, altered; and
> so the relations, proportions, values of each work of art toward
> the whole are readjusted; and this is conformity between the old
> and the new. Whoever has approved this idea of order, of the
> form of European, of English literature will not find it pre-
> posterous that the past should be altered by the present as much
> as the present is directed by the past.[2]

And the poet who strove constantly to escape sentimentality, "huge
gobs of raw sincerity," through irony and understatement, who
talked of the necessity of forcing "enthusiasm" through the "prism"
of metaphor, or who once wrote to Sidney Cox, "A subject has to
be held clear outside of me with struts and as it were set up for an
object. A subject must be an object" [3]—such a poetical theorist is
clearly akin to the Eliot who wrote, "Poetry is not a turning loose
of emotion, but an escape from emotion; it is not the expression of
personality, but an escape from personality." [4] And Frost, who
differentiated sharply between "griefs" and "grievances" would
also have agreed with Eliot's corollary: "But, of course, only those
who have personality and emotions know what it means to want
to escape from these things."

When Ezra Pound talks of "book words" as distinct from words
one could "actually say," when he asserts the importance of natural
speech rhythms and the avoidance of "emotional slither," [5] he is
reiterating, quite independently, one of Frost's most insistent critical
ideas. And if the blue-pencil job Frost does on Pound's "Portrait
D'une Femme" (Page 170) has less sense of critical sureness than

Pound's alterations of "The Waste Land," this is largely due to a particular quality of cantankerousness that blinded him to the merits of certain kinds of poetry. Certainly, other of Frost's incidental or marginal comments reflect a Poundian sharpness of insight.

Finally, if Frost's desire to get back to the soil—to contact with homely idioms and speech rhythms—has a more generalized artistic purpose than Yeats's, this is because he was not in a historical position to feel such contact as a national, as well as an artistic, urgency. But his determination to "think New Englandly," to fill his eclogues with New England characters and tones of voice, to demonstrate that, as with his beloved Roman poets, universality can rest on being truly provincial, has much in common with the Irish manifesto:

> John Synge, I and Augusta Gregory, thought
> All that we did, all that we said or sang
> Must come from contact with the soil, from that
> Contact everything Antaeus-like grew strong.[6]

Frost, then, in some of his basic critical presuppositions, is very much part of the most important early-twentieth-century theorizing. But with Frost a distinction needs to be made between the critical theorist and the practical critic. As a theorist, Frost was not only sophisticated; he was a self-conscious innovator, dedicated, practical, rather assertively aware of being "possibly the only person going who works on any but a worn out theory (principle I had better say) of versification."[7] Even if he was not in fact quite so original as he thought himself to be, this is the most rewarding part of Frost's criticism; he brings both integrity and sureness to it. His theories cover many aspects of poetry and have a flexibility that allows them to develop without losing their initial relevance. They range from his early ideas about sound, the "sound of sense," "voice-posturing," and a craftsman's concern for metrics, to a later, more abstract, conceptual awareness of language and a fascination with the meaning of meaning.

In between these extremes of the practical and the abstract, he turns his attention to such concerns as the act of creativity, methods of composition, the relation of poet to reader, the nature of originality, and the necessity for form. To be sure, his theories are rarely stated in formal terms—they occur incidentally in letters, prefaces, interviews, lectures—yet taken as a whole, they form one of the most significant bodies of poetical theory by any American poet, more profound and wide-ranging than Poe's, more practical and technical than Emerson's.

The practical critic falls far short of the theorist, and this is largely a problem of personality. Frost disliked formal critics. In part, perhaps, such dislike ties in with his basic intellectual suspicion of dogmatism, his sense of the need to hold ambiguities in flux. ("I'm afraid of too much structure. Some violence is always done to the wisdom you build a philosophy out of." [8]) This reservation is quite defensible, and fits in with the Romantic, and later the New Critical, avoidance of value judgments. In part, too, it fits in with his theory that the creative moment comes from a sense of "recognition," and that it is the poet's task to awaken a similar recognition in the reader: "If you feel it, let's just exchange glances and not say anything about it." [9] Recognition, like intuition, suffers from overexplication. But his dismissal of a critic like John Ciardi,[10] his irritability with the symbol hunters,[11] and his advice to Sidney Cox ("Let's not be too damned literary") all savor of the kind of aggressive defensiveness that one finds often in the amateur poet (who excuses basic ineptitude by a pose of taking his poetry neat, heart speaking to heart), but which one is surprised indeed to find in a poet of Frost's ability and sophistication. The irritability toward critics is present in the very tone of a letter to Lawrance Thompson about a proposed NBC broadcast:

> Besides the danger of seeing figures and symbols where none are intended is the dangerous presumption on the part of the critics that they can go the poet one better by telling him what he is up to. He may think he knows what he means but it takes a modern critic to catch him at what he is up to. Shelley for instance thought he meant the desire of the moth for the star when he was merely up to seduction. A little of the low-down on motivation goes a long way.[12]

There is no recognition whatsoever here, or anywhere else in Frost's writing, that a good critic can constructively elucidate a poem, that there is such a thing as creative criticism, or that a responsible critic can be an arbiter and preserver of those twin virtues of taste and judgment that Frost regarded as the true ends of a literary education.[13] More explicitly, there is here a flat rejection of the assumption that there can be "more" in a poem than the author is conscious of, that he can write better, more universally, than he knows; and so, by implication, the unconscious is dismissed as an area of creativity. Critics and poets are rivals, rarely allies.

Such antagonism can only be explained by the quirks of Frost's own personality, and these are evident in his biography. He himself admitted a strong feeling of jealousy toward potential rivals in poetry:

> Before I had published a book I was never conscious of the existence of any contemporary poet. But as soon as my first book came out, I became jealous of all of them—all but Robinson. Somehow I never felt jealous of him at any time.[14]

Frost obviously felt a strong sense of competitiveness. One of the saddest results of this was the negation of his wife's poetic talents; seemingly overshadowed by his artistic intensity, she even denied authorship of the poems she had written in high school.[15] Back of this jealousy and competitiveness lay an insecurity that seems strangely at odds with that confidence in his own talent that sustained him over twenty years of apprenticeship. Indeed this confidence never left him. The pride with which he rejected his publisher's suggestion that he publish *A Boy's Will* at his own expense, the fierce independence of his early dealings with Pound, and his aloofness from the poetic fads and fashions of the twenties and thirties all point to an artistic integrity and a consciousness of the poet's high role that is worthy of any Romantic. Yet the insecurity is plainly there, too. Time and again he turned down requests to write a review of a fellow poet, and his motives are unequivocal: "The very thought of reviewing scares me incoherent." [16] In 1916 he even rejected the opportunity to write an appreciation of Wilfred Gibson, with whom he had just been living in England, because "writing about writing is something I have never done nor wanted to do." [17]

His own craft, then, was one thing—he could, and did, expound

seriously on that in letters written from England and in lectures as
early as 1916—and he would use those principles as a basis of judging
other poets informally. But to abstract and formalize his critical
premises was quite another thing. He clearly separated these two
functions of criticism. His diffidence is perhaps most openly
expressed in the unpublished letter written to Norman Foerster
long after Frost had become an established poet:

> My dear Foerster:
> My debt to you is acknowledged. It is too great to be dealt
> with by telegraph. But ask me anything in payment except to
> act as a formal judge of poetry. It seems to me I spend half my
> time excusing myself from judgeships lately. I may tell you in
> confidence I refused to act on both the Pulitzer and Guggenheim
> committees of award—not without giving offense I was afraid.
> You I am sure will *take* no offense. I never set out in life to be
> a formal judge of anything. Judgement seems to fail me when it
> has to be formal. I suppose it becomes too conscientious. You will
> understand and indulge me.
>
> Sincerely yours
Robert Frost [18]
>
> South Shaftsbury Vt
> October 25 1931

And if an almost arrogant self-confidence seems oddly incompatible
with this profound sense of insecurity, other sensitive writers
have displayed the same combination. One has only to think of
Hawthorne's jealous guarding of his anonymity through his
years of apprenticeship; he too was a perfectionist, desperate for
reputation.

More important than the psychological reasons behind such
insecurity in Frost are the limitations that it imposes on his practical
criticism. There is the limitation of subject. He skirts the major
poetic figures of his time, indulging only in minor combat. One
would love to have his serious assessment of, for example, "The
Waste Land," "Hugh Selwyn Mauberley," "Four Quartets," or
the later Yeats, but one would search Frost's criticism in vain for
this. The most these poets get are incidental remarks, often obvious

or simplistic. Instead, for the most part, Frost concentrates his critical attention on minor contemporaries, peripheral figures at best, whom he cannot feel threatened by.

There is also the limitation of approach. Although he did honor Edwin Arlington Robinson posthumously with a prose preface to Robinson's *King Jasper*, Frost rarely honors criticism itself with a shape so formal. That preface, he later admitted, cost him "a great deal" ("I am not a practiced prose writer" [19]). Most of his practical criticism, like his critical theories, occurs offhandedly—in letters, marginalia, conversations, or interviews. The often playful freedom that such informality affords also restricts our acceptance of his judgments. Which of his various opinions of Amy Lowell's poetry, for example, represents his definitive critical stand? When is he simply spoofing his correspondent, or working out a certain temporary peevishness in himself? When does tact cut across truthfulness? Or vindictiveness prevent wholeness of judgment? Or playfulness sidetrack seriousness? The question of tone in the individual piece thus becomes important; letters need to be checked against each other and the truth of a particular critical stance extracted from a kaleidoscope of moods. Certain correspondents, of course, are more reliable than others. Friends like John Bartlett, Sidney Cox, or Louis Untermeyer tend to get the "total" Frost, often speculative and uncertain; a more censored version goes to critics like William Braithwaite or Amy Lowell—they get only what Frost wants them to get.

Yet within these limitations, Frost's practical criticism remains valuable. What it lacks in ambition, and seriousness, and broad sweep, it almost makes up for in fine discrimination, and particularity, and attention to craftsmanship. It gives an added insight into his own poetry, and helps us to place it realistically beside both the achievement of his contemporaries and the American poetic heritage to which he was so much committed.

FROST AS A CRITICAL THEORIST

> They would not find me changed from him they knew—
> Only more sure of all I thought was true.

Despite Robert Frost's assertion of this dubious virtue, his ideas about poetry did change; at least the expression of them did. Although the central idea of the importance of the speaking voice remained with him, the language in which he talked about his poetry changed over the years from the technical ("tones," "voice-posture," "metrics") to the moral and psychological ("belief," "commitment," "courage," "prowess") and to the linguistic ("meaning," "metaphor," "naming"). His early critical ideas were wholly those of the craftsman; later ideas were those of the philosopher. A quality of abstraction creeps in—the result not simply of age, or fame, or rationalization, but of a broader concern for the nature and function of poetry.

The heritage of poetic form against which Frost formulated his earliest ideas was the musical assonance of most nineteenth-century poetry. Poetry and music were seen as twin offspring of the same Victorian muse. Frost set out to wrench them apart. In a letter to John Bartlett in 1913 he explained:

> You see the great successes in recent poetry have been made on the assumption that the music of words was a matter of harmonised vowels and consonants. Both Swinburne and Tennyson arrived largely at effects in assonation. But they were on the wrong track or at any rate on a short track. They went the length of it. Any one else who goes that way must go after them. And that's where most are going. [Page 58]

Frost, seeking a road less traveled by, began with a certainty that poetry was, in its essence, different from music. A light exchange with Louis Untermeyer indicates his irritation at any blurring of these two separate art forms. "Tell me, Louis," he wrote in 1915, "while it is uppermost in my mind what, when you are doing the high critical, do you mean by 'overtones' in poetry." At Untermeyer's presumably reassuring reply that it meant nothing, Frost's relief is obvious: "It's all right then. . . . It's just one of those bad analogies that obliterates the distinction between poetry and music." [1]

This suspiciousness toward musicality, then, was a basic starting premise—though Frost was not as alone in holding it as he imagined. Yeats, though his early poetry would appear to deny it, was asserting the same distinction [2] and advising John Synge to go to the west of Ireland and listen to people talk. The anthology *Georgian Poetry: 1911–1912* declared its separation from *fin-de-siècle* musicality and a return to natural speech rhythms. Yet Frost's position as an American poet gave him a somewhat different perspective. American poetry in the nineteenth century had polarized itself more obviously than English poetry. One of the poles had been Edgar Allan Poe, who in "The Rationale of Verse" claimed that verse "cannot be better designated than an inferior or less capable music," [3] and whose own poetry surrendered all other poetic effects to the lulling hypnosis of sound. This tradition continued through much minor poetry to later poets like Sidney Lanier and Vachel Lindsay, both of whom Frost rejected vigorously. When "My Butterfly" was first published in *The Independent* in 1894, the well-meaning editor sent Frost a copy of Lanier's verse so that he could study felicity of meter. Frost's refusal to do so ("No writer has ever been corrected into importance") was a declaration that his poetic aims were different. And all his life he scoffed at the orchestrations and stage directions of Vachel Lindsay: " 'Say this in a golden tone,' he says. You ought not to have to say that in the margin. . . . That ought to be in the meaning." (Page 156) One of his few parodies has Lindsay as its target. (Page 167)

Running a strong countermovement to this poetry-as-music tradition in nineteenth-century America is a colloquial tradition, to which in fact the best poets belonged: Emerson, with his imperfect rhymes and meters, calling for "not metres, but a metre-making argument," Whitman, with his use of slang and free rhythm, Emily Dickinson whose homely diction and frequent metrical irregularity give the impression of a speaking voice, and Edwin Arlington Robinson whose "talking tones" Frost so much admired. This was the tradition, virtually closed to the Georgians, that Frost was heir to. As he dogmatically summed it up in a lecture years later: "No music is the same as poetry, any more than architecture and poetry is [sic] the same." [4]

Although poetry for Frost was not "an inferior and less capable music," yet for him its essence lay, constructively and meaningfully, in sound. He was no Imagist. For him sound was the great artistic catalyst, and its function was mysteriously epistemological. As early as 1894 he made this extraordinary statement in a letter: "Sound is an element of poetry, one but for which the imagination would become reason." [5] Thus, whereas Wordsworth, for example, would talk of the imagination in terms of encounters, direct or remembered, with the physical world, and Emerson in terms of neo-Platonic glimpses of reality, Frost talks of it in terms of prosody, of what he never ceased to regard as the central feature of poetry. The physical perception dictates the emotional one:

> There are only three things, after all, that a poem must reach: the eye, the ear, and what we may call the heart or the mind. It is the most important of all to reach the heart of the reader. And the surest way to reach the heart is through the ear. The visual images thrown up by a poem are important, but it is more important still to choose and arrange words in a sequence so as virtually to control the intonations and pauses of the reader's voice. By the arrangement and choice of words on the part of the poet, the effects of humor, pathos, hysteria, anger, and in fact, all effects, can be indicated or obtained. [6]

If this initially appears close to Poe, the distinction lies in Frost's characterization of sound as being "the intonations and pauses of the reader's voice." Not the rhythmic, singing, voice, but the talking voice. Most of Frost's early critical ideas center on this concept.

In later years, he was fond of recalling how this theory crystallized for him. A clergyman friend, commenting on Frost's first poem in *The Independent*, tried to give him some advice about metrics, as the poem sounded too much like talking. Suddenly Frost knew precisely what he was after: the sound of talk. But his fascination with this was always more prosodic than picturesque or cultural. He was not interested in idioms and intonations for their quaintness, or their national or local flavor. Although he admired Synge, he himself would never, as he told Sidney Cox, have listened to conversations through a chink in the ceiling and written down notes,[7] and this difference in literary approach is reflected in the difference in artistic effects. The rich language of Synge's plays is a *distillation* of images and rhythms heard, in fact a highly literary language—"as fully flavoured as a nut or an apple." [8] It is Frost's undoctored language that actually gives us the sense of eavesdropping. He sought to extend the boundaries of literature into the real vernacular, whose meaning was as varied as the tones of voice that could be used to express it:

> There are two kinds of language: the spoken language and the written language—our every day speech which we call the vernacular; and a more literary, sophisticated, artificial, elegant language that belongs to books. We often hear it said that a man talks like a book in this second way. We object to anybody's talking in this literary, artificial English; we don't object to anybody's writing in it; we rather expect people to write in a literary, somewhat artificial style. I, myself, could get along very well without this bookish language altogether.[8] [Page 145]

A proper understanding of intonation, the sense of the speaking voice, opened up to Frost endless possibilities for poetic effects. At the furthest extreme, intonation alone could carry meaning, quite divorced from particular words. Frost was fond of citing the example of listening to the rise and fall of voices behind closed doors or just out of earshot, where individual words could not be discerned, yet meaning, emotion, and dramatic interaction could all be intuited. Similarly, he had a Celtic delight in listening to the limited vocabulary of hearty curses and the infinite variety of meanings they could convey, depending solely "on the tones of saying it and the situations." But intonations conveyed most when they occurred most naturally, as interdependent with the actual

words, when the voice itself could add connotative to denotative
meaning.

This interdependence Frost called "sound-posturing": the tone
of voice extended, even perhaps created, the "dictionary" meaning
of a word or phrase. At the same time, one could only know how
to say a particular sentence by an understanding of the total
meaning, or context. Language is a living, dramatic thing and
communication depends largely on the performer:

> I say you cant read a single good sentence with the salt in it
> unless you have previously heard it spoken. Neither can you
> with the help of all the characters and diacritical marks pro-
> nounce a single word unless you have previously heard it actually
> pronounced. Words exist in the mouth not in books. You can't
> fix them and you dont want to fix them. You want them to adapt
> their sounds to persons and places and times. You want them to
> change and be different. [Page 62]

Not every yawp, then, had to be barbaric. Frost's own favorite
example was the almost endless variety of meaning possible in the
simple word "Oh":

> "Take, for instance, the expression 'oh.' The American poets
> use it in practically one tone, that of grandeur: 'Oh Soul!' 'Oh
> Hills!'—'Oh Anything!' That's the way they go. But think of
> what 'oh' is really capable: the 'oh' of scorn, the 'oh' of amuse-
> ment, the 'oh' of surprise, the 'oh' of doubt—and there are many
> more." [9]

The particular tone chosen—whether of scorn, or amusement, or
surprise, or doubt—will be dictated by the dramatic situation of the
speaker. This is what Frost worked hard to establish through context in his own poetry. He once told Sidney Cox that he added the
moral at the end of "The Runaway" just for the pleasure of the
aggrieved tone of voice,[10] and in a letter to John Cournos it is in
the achievement of this "hearing imagination" that he takes most
pride:

I also think well of those four "don'ts" in Home Burial. They would be good in prose and they gain something from the way they are placed in the verse. Then there is the threatening
             "If—you—do!" (Last of Home Burial)
     It is that particular kind of imagination that I cultivate rather than the kind that merely sees things, the hearing imagination rather than the seeing imagination though I should not want to be without the latter.
     I am not bothered by the question whether anyone will be able to hear or say those three words ("If—you—do!") as I mean them to be said or heard. I should say that they were sufficiently self expressive. Some doubt that such tones can long survive on paper. They'll probably last as long as the finer meanings of words.[11]

After Frost had thus broadened the poetic possibilities of individual words by such concentration on the relation of sound to meaning, it was but a small step to extend the flexibility of the sentence, to wage war on the traditional concept of the sentence as "a grammatical cluster of words," and to establish instead "the distinction between the grammatical sentence and the vital sentence." (Page 67) Again, it was a matter of intonation, of voice posture: "There's something in the living sentence (in the shape of it) that is more important than any phrasing or chosen word." [12] The best analysis of this idea occurs in the letters to John Bartlett and Sidney Cox (Pages 63 and 67). What is curious, however, in view of Frost's usual insistence on the possibilities, rather than the limitations, of intonational effect is his frequent claim that there are only a certain fixed number of sentence-sounds in man's vocal run:

Remember, a certain fixed number of sentences (sentence sounds) belong to the human throat just as a certain fixed number of vocal runs belong to the throat of a given kind of bird. These are fixed I say. Imagination can not create them. It can only call them up.[13]

The physical possibilities for expression, which so extend the meanings of words and sentences, in the end, it would seem, also mark their limitations. As Frost wrote to John Freeman: "The brute tones of our human throat [,] that may once have been all our meaning. I suppose there is one for every feeling we shall ever feel, yes and for every thought we shall ever think. Such is the limitation of our thought." (Page 80) Art consists not in creating new variations (for that would place the artist outside nature) but in listening for tones that have not been stereotyped by literary expression, in collecting and arranging. Appreciation rests in recognition, not discovery.

The very images of orchestration, of stage direction, with which Frost talks of gathering and selecting his sentence-arrangements indicate how close his conception of poetry is to drama. He wrote only three complete plays (if one includes the two masques), yet he conducted a lifelong flirtation with the stage. During his first teaching appointment at Pinkerton Academy, he produced five plays, ranging from *The Rivals* to *Cathleen ni Houlihan;* throughout his life, he seized any opportunity he could to attend plays; certain of his dramatic eclogues were formally dramatized and acted.[14] His statements on writing continually affirm this quality: "Everything written is as good as it is dramatic. It need not declare itself in form, but it is drama or nothing." [15] He has expressed his indebtedness to Turgenev. Indeed, his realization of the innate dramatic possibilities of stasis ("It is a poem just to mention driving into a strange barn to bide the passing of a thunder storm" [16]) has much in common with Chekov or Maeterlinck; "An Old Man's Winter Night" is just such a "play." Like these dramatists, he was acutely aware not only of the dramatic force of intonations, but also of pauses and silences. Hence the importance of the pauses in "If—you—do!" And hence the superb control of inarticulateness, of silences and breakings-off, in "A Servant to Servants." At a time when Ibsen was revolutionizing the nineteenth-century drama with thesis-plays ("writing from a formula," Frost told Sidney Cox), and later, when Shaw's argumentative prefaces covered more space than his actual plays, Frost's notion of the real source of dramatic interest never wavered. Language, properly conveyed, contained its own conflicts. He went back to Shakespeare to justify his "sound of sense." Real drama did not come from imposed theses, or extravagant stage directions, not even from body movement. His appreciation of a play by Edwin Arlington Robinson is typical: "The speaking tones are all there on the printed page, nothing is left for the actor but to recognize and give them. And the action is in the speech where it should be, and not along beside it in antics for the body to perform." (Page 94) This is the concept of "language as gesture" indeed. In fact, quite early Frost defined literature to Louis Untermeyer as "words that have become deeds." [17]

Because Frost's sense of drama, as of poetry, was so tied to this "language such as men do use," his themes belong strictly to the here and now. If Poe in *Politian* shifted the Kentucky Beauchamp murder case to sixteenth-century Rome, the strange transmigration was surely due as much to the lack of an adequate language to cope with the local and present as it was to his natural penchant for the exotic. Frost's English friend Lascelles Abercrombie, publishing the first act of his play *The Sale of St. Thomas* in 1911, was careful to set it at a distance—India, at the time of Christ; and again one suspects on his part a failure of language. Frost's "dramas," on the other hand, even when they are about witches, are about witches actually known in the present, like the witch of Coös. Similarly, part of what makes *A Masque of Reason* such a stylistic tour de force is that the philosophical dilemma is couched in the language of colloquial American rationalism. In a revealing letter to John Erskine, Frost states clearly his attitude toward arbitrary objectification. Commenting on a poem by Erskine, he concludes:

> But why to objectify the idea and put it far enough away from yourself must you put it away off in antiquity and say it in heroes and gods. Why must you every time, I mean. All right for this poem; but why not next time say it in modern people. It is like diffidence, shyness, this remoteness in time and space. Get over it and you can break in on the age with your strength and insight. [Page 100]

By the time he went to England in 1912, Frost's basic ideas about poetry were already established. The seriousness and self-consciousness with which he formulated them are affirmed not only in his letters at this time but also by his eagerness to discuss his ideas among the friends he found in the new literary world that was opening up to him. The world of literary camaraderie and exchange of ideas had been denied him in the years at Derry; he now, though not without some reservations in regard to certain of his fellow poets, took advantage of his new opportunities. In an unpublished postcard to F. S. Flint, Frost solicits the advice of Flint and T. E. Hulme:

> Do you suppose you could get Hulme to listen with you some night to my theory of what would be pure form in poetry? I don't want to talk to a salon, but to a couple of clear-heads who will listen and give my idea its due. I will be greatly helped in what is before me by a little honest criticism. You would advise as metrical expert and he as philosopher. Do I ask too much.
>
>   R. Frost
> Be sure not to force Hulme. I wouldn't put him to sleep for the world.[18]

This meeting took place, and Frost was obviously grateful for the chance to articulate his critical theories. He referred to the meeting in a letter written the following week:

> I don't know but that I have delivered the best of what I had to say on the sound of sense. What more there may be I will be on hand to talk over with you and Hulme at five, Tuesday. My ideas got just the rub they needed last week. [Page 83]

The same self-consciousness underlies the tone of conviction with which Frost wrote to Sidney Cox in 1914 about the Poet Laureate. Bridges' syllabic theories, according to Frost, were not only unsuited to a naturally accentual language like English, but they closed the door to all the dramatic possibilities of intonation, everything that makes a poem "living" as distinct from the "dead" poetry of extinct languages that are revived only in formalized scansion:

> The living part of a poem is the intonation entangled somehow in the syntax idiom and meaning of a sentence. It is only there

for those who have heard it previously in conversation. It is not for us in any Greek or Latin poem because our ears have not been filled with the tones of Greek and Roman talk. It is the most volatile and at the same time important part of poetry. It goes and the language becomes a dead language, the poetry dead poetry. [Page 61]

It was surely of this intonation that Frost was thinking when he later described poetry as "that which is lost out of both prose and verse in translation." (Page 159)

Central as this concept of "voice-posture" or "sound of sense" was to Frost's critical thought, however, he was not naïve enough to think that the capturing of tones of voice was anything more than the "raw material" of poetry. He was no simple tape recorder. And he was constantly at pains to dissociate himself from free-versers like Carl Sandburg. If a proper ear for intonation increased one's awareness of the range of natural rhythm and accent in English, this was just the beginning: "An ear and an appetite for these sounds of sense is the first qualification of a writer, be it of prose or verse. But if one is to be a poet he must learn to get cadences by skilfully breaking the sounds of sense with all their irregularity of accent across the regular beat of the metre." (Page 59)

Talking of capturing the sentence tones of everyday talk, he notes:

No one makes them or adds to them. They are always there— living in the cave of the mouth. They are real cave things: they were before words were. And they are as definitely things as any image of sight. The most creative imagination is only their summoner. But summoning them is not all. They are only lovely when thrown and drawn and displayed across spaces of the footed line.[19]

The rather self-conscious mixture here of the image of the magician with that of the craftsman suggests the duality behind poetic creation.

There has always been a particularly close relation between poetic meter and poetic meaning.[20] The very earliest poets knew that the regular stress of meter gives poetry a definite emotional, even a physical appeal. All of us, Frost often said, grew up on Mother Goose; and nursery rhymes have had their perennial appeal simply through our instinctual reaction to a regular beat. Yet the best poets have also known that too much regularity is soporific, or can lead to doggerel; and their real craftsmanship has lain in constructing irregularities within some chosen framework. Rhythm and meter had to be wary bedfellows. Frost's theory carries this idea even further. Since he had enlarged the concept of natural speaking rhythms by his capturing of intonations, there is, accordingly, a greater sense of conflict in the way meter tries to harness these rhythms. Note the imagery of strain that is always present when Frost talks of poetic creation: "I am never more pleased than when I can get these into strained relation. I like to drag and break the intonation across the meter as waves first comb and then break stumbling on the shingle." [21] Forty years later, this sense of strain was still obviously the most conscious part of Frost's craftsmanship: "They use the word 'rhythm' about a lot of free verse; and gee, what's the good of the rhythm unless it is on something that trips it—that it ruffles? You know, it's got to ruffle the meter." (Page 156)

For the poet who wrote "West-Running Brook," this basic conflict in the act of creation, this sense of art won only through strain, was symptomatic of profounder conflicts. Frost's kind of poetry mirrored basic psychological oppositions; and his art, in this sense, was truly mimetic. In a short casual letter he mentioned the idea in passing: "Free rhythms are as disorderly as nature; meters are as orderly as human nature and take their rise in rhythms just as human nature rises out of nature." [22]

To Frost, form is as necessary to poetry as the discipline of holding opposites in flux is necessary to the emotional life; and for the same reasons. Hence his sweeping statements on the human relevance of poetry. Insanity in his own family gave him enough evidence to fear the lack of such inner structure. Not surprisingly, then, he talks of form in two ways. When he hurls abuse at the "free-versters," "form" has a purely technical meaning; it embraces the traditional poetic tools of selectivity, choice of words, meter, and stanzaic patterning. His favorite comparison here was that writing free verse was like playing tennis with the net down—no fun, no challenge, no effect. "There is no greater fallacy going," he wrote to Sidney Cox, "than that art is expression—an undertaking to tell all to the last scrapings of the brain pan. . . . My object is true form . . . form true to any chance bit of true life." [23] And he lightheartedly asserts the importance of "measure" in the poem "The Aim Was Song." But even quite early in his theorizing, form also had a broader, more philosophical meaning; it is this meaning, associated with concepts like "freedom," and "belief," and "performance," that came to predominate in Frost's later attitudes. "Form" was a way of encompassing and giving coherence to the confusion and chaos of life itself; this imposed discipline then liberated one to a truer "freedom"—"the almost incredible freedom of the soul enslaved to the hard facts of experience," [24] as he expressed it to Edward Garnett in 1915 while giving his definition of "realist." Frost's idea of form was never dilettantish nor purely theoretical. He welcomed the confusions and crudities of experience precisely because of this opportunity for conflict; in an almost existential sense, one defined oneself through the tussle. "I thank the Lord for crudity," he wrote, "which is rawness, which is raw material, which is the part of life not yet worked up into form, or at least not worked all the way up." [25] He wanted the world no different from what it was: "I wouldn't give a cent to see the world . . . made better. . . . I have no quarrel with the material." [26] As the surprisingly orthodox theology of *A Masque of Reason* affirms:

> Except as a hard place to save his soul in,
> A trial ground where he can try himself
> And find out whether he is any good,
> It would be meaningless. It might as well
> Be Heaven at once and have it over with. [27]

Frost was thus a realist in the most experiential sense, and form was sheer tough-mindedness. He shrewdly saw through the phony, yet immensely popular, "realism" of Edgar Lee Masters, for example, claiming that Masters was "too romantic for my taste, and by romantic I'm afraid I mean among other things false-realistic." [28]

His own resolution of the confrontation with the "crudity" of experience was usually the more controlled one of ironic understatement.

But if "form" thus acts as a catalyst in this philosophical resolution of "crudity," it is also a paradigm of such resolution. In the terminology of *A Masque of Reason*, art can capture the "meaning" only if it echoes the sense of "trial"; the very *form* of a poem must emerge from a confrontation with the "threat" of formlessness. Thus, as Frost wrote to Sidney Cox as early as 1914: "[O]ur technique becomes as much material as material itself." (Page 68) In the series of teasing questions that he puts to Lewis Chase (Page 73), he asks twice if his poems produce a feeling of threat; and in a letter to Amy Bonner written many years later he relates form directly to both life and art, and asserts the necessity of threat to both:

[T]here are no two things as important to us in life and art as being threatened and being saved. What are ideals of form for if we arent going to be made to fear for them? All our ingenuity is lavished on getting into danger legitimately so that we may be genuinely rescued. [Page 76]

Twelve years earlier, Frost had expressed in a memorable image an idea similar to this precarious, nonlinear "progress" through "being threatened and being saved":

The most exciting movement in nature is not progress, advance, but expansion and contraction, the opening and shutting of the eye, the hand, the heart, the mind. We throw our arms wide with a gesture of religion to the universe; we close them around a person. We explore and adventure for a while and then we draw in to consolidate our gains. The breathless swing is between subject matter and form. [Page 136]

One feature of form that bridges the technical and philosophical meanings is style, and Frost, in a letter to Untermeyer, gives a thoughtful analysis of this (Page 77), which he later expanded in his Preface to *King Jasper*. Style, he notes, is "that which indicates how the writer takes himself and what he is saying. . . . It is the mind skating circles round itself as it moves forward." It thus establishes the necessary objectivity, the judgment of the intellect on the emotional involvement of artistic creation. Most difficult, because most intangible, of all qualities for the artist to develop, it is nevertheless the ultimate pointer to his literary tact and literary faith. The easiest escape is to be completely abstract, to have no style at all. Frost thus criticizes one of Amy Lowell's poems: "How completely outside of herself she gets and how completely outside of everybody else she keeps. She executes a frightfulness." [29] Elinor Wylie, on the other hand, at least establishes an attitude to her subject in a kind of irony, and the presence of "style" wins his approval:

> She was self-conscious artist enough to see her appointed task. It was to make a false heart ring false. Art forbade that a false heart should ring true. That would have been false art. The rules of the game permitted her, required her, to slip from one pose to its opposite even in the same poem when of moderate length. So long as she kept her high poetic strain, so long as the work was all crystals, sugar, glass, semi-precious and precious, the falser she was the truer she rang. The ultimate test is how a writer takes himself as betrayed in tone, word-font, and collateral advertising. I find the Wylie's way of taking herself, her airs about herself, not very detestable.[30]

Irony, he realizes, is simply "self-defence," just as humor is. And Frost should know. In the same letter to Untermeyer on style, he goes on: "I own any form of humor shows fear and inferiority. Irony is simply a kind of guardedness. . . . Humor is the most engaging cowardice. With it myself I have been able to hold some of my enemy in play far out of gunshot." The best writers, those who dare, take their beliefs seriously: "Belief is better than anything else, and it is best when rapt, above paying its respects to anybody's doubt whatsoever." For Frost, the best example of such commitment was Emerson.

Belief, then. But this should not be confused with beliefs, particularly the social and political credos that rang through the 1920's, just as griefs should not be confused with grievances. For belief meant acceptance of the age for the possibilities it offered, a sense of the eternal verities. "We have no way of knowing that this age is one of the worst in the world's history," he wrote to *The Amherst Student* in 1935. ". . . It is immodest of a man to think of himself as going down before the worst forces ever mobilized by God." (Page 112) Life, like poetry, finds not only its security but also its triumph in form. He concludes the same letter with Faulknerian tolling: "The background is hugeness and confusion shading away from where we stand into black and utter chaos; and against the background any small man-made figure of order and concentration."

Frost's definitions of poetry in the middle years of his career have thus left behind the technical questions of intonations and rhythms and meters, and concern themselves instead with this sense of metaphysical struggle. "Every poem," he wrote in 1946, "is an epitome of the great predicament; a figure of the will braving alien entanglements." (Page 130) In a jocular letter to Leonidas Payne as early as 1927, he made a revealing metaphor out of a childhood incident:

> My poems . . . are all set to trip the reader head foremost into the boundless. Ever since infancy I have had the habit of leaving my blocks carts chairs and such like ordinaries where people would be pretty sure to fall forward over them in the dark. Forward, you understand, *and* in the dark.[31]

And perhaps his most sustained and famous metaphor for poetry occurs in "The Figure a Poem Makes," the preface he wrote to his collected poems in 1939:

> It begins in delight and ends in wisdom. The figure is the same as for love. No one can really hold that the ecstasy should be static and stand still in one place. It begins in delight, it inclines to the impulse, it assumes direction with the first line laid down, it runs a course of lucky events, and ends in a clarification of life—not necessarily a great clarification, such as sects and cults are founded on, but in a momentary stay against confusion. [Page 126]

It would be foolish to try to establish a strict chronological scheme in relation to Frost's critical theories. Sheer technique continued to interest him throughout his life, and there are slight hints of a more philosophical approach even in his earliest statements. But there is, from about 1925 on, a definite shift in emphasis, a change in expression and therefore in concept. The correspondence of poetry and life, of the technical and metaphysical meanings of form, occupied him increasingly. The position given to literature in the Platonic ladder of Frost's famous "four beliefs" is significant: self-belief, the belief of love, literary belief, and belief in God.[32] Not only is literature seen quite specifically here as a matter of "belief," but the nature of that belief is defined by what circumscribes it; it takes off from the human and points to the infinite; it is indeed "the will braving alien entanglements." The Biblical cadences into which Frost's prose often falls are not altogether fortuitous; there was a little of the prophet in Frost's own "style." If "form" liberated one to "freedom," freedom was "nothing but departure," and the creative possibilities were staggering. What mattered, as he came more and more to extract himself from his material, was "performance," the self-definition achieved by means of technical mastery.

Certainly, when Frost discussed the nature of poetic creation, he never belittled the initial inspiration—the "mood" or "moment" as he often called it. A "performance" can hardly take place in a vacuum; it must have material to shape. He never really analyzed the "moment," simply accepting it like a moment of grace or intuition. In a much-quoted extract from a letter to Louis Untermeyer, Frost enlarges the idea:

A poem is never a put-up job so to speak. It begins as a lump in the throat, a sense of wrong, a homesickness, a lovesickness. It is never a thought to begin with. It is at its best when it is a tantalizing vagueness. It finds its thought and succeeds, or doesn't find it and comes to nothing. It finds its thought or makes its thought. I suppose it finds it lying around with others not so much to its purpose in a more or less full mind. That's why it oftener comes to nothing in youth before experience has filled the mind with thoughts. It may be a big big emotion then and yet finds nothing it can embody in. It finds the thought and the thought finds the words. Let's say again: A poem particularly must not begin with thought first.[33]

Actually this was simplifying his practice a little. In a subtle analysis of Frost's poetic impulse, Lawrance Thompson sees it more accurately as a two-way operation: sometimes Frost did work from an initial emotion through to thought by way of metaphor (as in "Stopping by Woods"), but at other times (as in "For Once, Then, Something") he starts with a sudden mental perception and, working it out through analogy, reaches an emotional afterglow.[34] But the emphasis, even in that letter to Untermeyer, is on the working out. The "performance" was an act of clarification, and one of its greatest dangers was "facility," a slickness that denied the difficulty of the performance. At the same time, for Frost a poem could not be "worried into existence." Some revisions were always possible and usually necessary, but if a poem did not find its essential form at the beginning, he usually set it aside. There was only one right way of saying a thing:

> I have never been good at revising. I always thought I made things worse by recasting and retouching. I never knew what was meant by choice of words. It was one word or none. When I saw more than one possible way of saying a thing I knew I was fumbling and turned from writing. If I ever fussed a poem into shape I hated and distrusted it afterward. The great and pleasant memories are of poems that were single strokes (one stroke to the poem) carried through. I won't say I haven't learned with the years something of the tinker's art. I'm surprised to find sometimes how I have just missed the word. It wasn't that I was groping for my meaning. I had that clear enough and I had thought I had said the word for it. But I hadn't said within a row of apple trees of it.[35]

It is Frost's interest in the nature of the clarification-through-performance that marks a third stage in his critical thinking. From his early preoccupation with the technical aspects of poetry, and from his later more philosophical interest in the relation of poetry to life, Frost became increasingly fascinated by such questions as the meaning of meaning, the nature of metaphor and of originality, the relation of poet to reader—the broad epistemological questions that put him very much in the stream of modern linguistic philosophy. Again, the time lines are, to say the least, blurred. These were not consecutive "developments" in a rising scale of critical value; they are simply the shiftings of interest that one might expect in a long career. Nor is this last phase even as clearly defined as the other two; it is stated or implied, with varying degrees of formality, over many years.

Frost was always concerned with the nature of poetic communication; he wanted to "get the poems over" to a general public, having no desire to be, as he considered Pound was, "caviare to the crowd." In discussing this communication, he uses the same words— "remembering," "recognition"—to indicate the poem's effect on both the poet and the reader. For the poet, the poem takes off from the realization of "delight," like the sudden apprehension of love:

> No tears in the writer, no tears in the reader. No surprise for the writer, no surprise for the reader. For me the initial delight is in the surprise of remembering something I didn't know I knew. I am in a place, in a situation, as if I had materialized from cloud or risen out of the ground. There is a glad recognition of the long lost and the rest follows. [Page 126]

For the reader the effect must be the same: "The artist's object is to tell people what they haven't as yet realized they were about to say themselves." [36] Or, as Frost expressed it to John Bartlett as early as 1914:

> A word about recognition: In literature it is our business to give people the thing that will make them say, "Oh yes I know what you mean." It is never to tell them something they dont know, but something they know and hadnt thought of saying. It must be something they recognize. [Page 64]

A poem will achieve this only if it has been a genuine act of clarification for the poet—not a "formula" poem that works up to a previously selected felicitous last line—and if the clarification takes place within the framework of the poem itself. Thus Frost was impatient with transient poetic vogues, originality for the sake of originality, "new ways to be new." The problem was the age-old one of understanding, beyond the limited clarification of debate. "I have wanted to find ways to transcend the strife-method," he wrote to Sidney Cox. "I have found some. . . . It is not so much anti-conflict as it is something beyond conflict. . . . I'll bet I could tell of spiritual realizations that for the moment at least would overawe the contentious. . . . Every poem is one." [37] What was essential for him was that the "act of clarification" remain fluid. It is possible to think out a perception totally before writing, in which case the poem has been thought out of existence. Or the technique of a poem can become too insistent and take over the initial "recognition": "What counts is the amount of the original intention that isnt turned back in execution." [38] In a good poem the poet discovers his world as he creates it in language; he is the "happy discoverer of his ends."

Thus the language itself has to be a discovery. Clichés and jaded diction carry no insight because they freeze meaning, allowing the mind no new "feats of association." In a perceptive statement on *Spoon River Anthology*, Frost touches on the relation of diction to originality:

> But I can't say for certain that I don't like Spoon River. I believe I do like it in a way. . . . I could wish it weren't so nearly the ordinary thing in its attitude toward respectability. How shall we treat respectability? That is not for me to say: I am not treating it. All I know with any conviction is that an idea has to be a little new to be at all true and if you say a thing three times it ceases to be so. [39]

Frost himself sought "the unmade words to work with, not the familiar made ones that everybody exclaims Poetry! at." (Page 68) On March 13, 1918, he gave a talk to a class of boys at the Browne and Nichols School that he entitled "The Unmade Word, or Fetching and Far-fetching"; in it he urged that words should be "fetched" from one association and moved to another place, given another extension of meaning, in order to keep a language fresh. This fear of clichés in itself is not unusual; most good poets have been concerned with poetry as "the renewal of words." But Frost explores the nature of language, and the relation of naming to meaning, much more abstractly in the poem "Maple."

A girl called Maple is plagued from her schooldays by the difference her name has imposed on her. Other names—like the Mabel she is taken for—mean nothing, are simply denotative. Hers had "too much meaning" and her search for whatever the meaning was becomes a search for an identity, her self-seeking:

> Her problem was to find out what it asked
> In dress or manner of the girl who bore it.

The word thus exerts a deterministic, shaping force on her experience. She looks for an unequivocal explanation—but the page in the Bible marked by a maple leaf tells her nothing, and her father's anecdote about her naming is ambiguous, belonging only to *his* experience. So absolute truth is ruled out, and human truth is proved relative. Eventually, through the intuition of a fresh perception rather than through a passive acceptance of a given correspondence, a man understands her meaning:

> "Do you know you remind me of a tree—
> A maple tree?"
>
>   "Because my name is Maple?"
>
> "Isn't it Mabel? I thought it was Mabel."
>
> "No doubt you've heard the office call me Mabel.
> I have to let them call me what they like."
>
> They were both stirred that he should have divined
> Without the name her personal mystery.
> It made it seem as if there must be something
> She must have missed herself.

Together they make one final trip to her birth-place to see if there, at the place of origin, they can locate the experience that gave rise to the name. Seemingly at a dead-end,

> They clung to what one had seen in the other
> By inspiration. It proved there was something.

Yet even then, faced with simply the *existence* of the name, lacking the history that went into the creating of it, they can still choose, from the immediacy of their own experiences, the connotations that will provide their own "meaning." So "they kept their thought away from when the maples/ Stood uniform in buckets," and associated her instead with "the tree the autumn fire ran through/ And swept of leathern leaves." Suddenly one final revelation is offered to them in a striking image of visual parallel:

> Once they came on a maple in a glade,
> Standing alone with smooth arms lifted up,
> And every leaf of foliage she'd worn
> Laid scarlet and pale pink about her feet.

But "discovery" is prevented by their lack of "faith":

> They hovered for a moment near discovery,
> Figurative enough to see the symbol,
> But lacking faith in anything to mean
> The same at different times to different people.
> Perhaps a filial diffidence partly kept them
> From thinking it could be a thing so bridal.

Caught thus in the self-imposed trap of relative thinking, they are finally blinded to further insights by their deliberate halting of the active quest:

> "We would not see the secret if we could now:
> We are not looking for it any more."

It is a curious poem. It borders on the tall tale, yet the tone is more perplexed than facetious, and the very "tallness" of the narrative only highlights the deeper "meanings" of the poem in which, as in "Birches," "Truth . . . with all her matter of fact" is set beside Truth as interpretation, as discovery, as experience, as metaphor. The poem thus explores some profound and complex ideas about the nature of knowledge, language, and personality. Who gave meaning to the name? The previous generation ("Something between your father and your mother/ Not meant for us at all")? The girl's own experience? The "inspiration" of her husband, creating fresh metaphoric relevance? Or the gratuitous revelation of the tree at the end, offering, in true Emersonian fashion, new correspondences? How does meaning shape experience? Or experience create meaning? If Frost here seems in the realm of I. A. Richards and Wittgenstein, this does not necessarily mean that he had read either of them. His puzzling about the nature of language, and the relation of "Nature" to language, goes back rather to Emerson, but the nature of his preoccupations here place him in the same arena as some of the more sophisticated critical theorists of the twentieth century.

Central to Frost's thinking about the meaning of meaning are his ideas on metaphor. One of the most striking features of his prose from the very beginning is that nearly all his attempts at explanation or definition lead him into metaphor:

I like to drag and break the intonation across the meter as waves first comb and then break stumbling on the shingle.

[A poem] begins in delight and ends in wisdom. The figure is the same as for love.

[Style] is the mind skating circles round itself as it moves forward.

In the *Paris Review* interview he told Richard Poirier: "Every thought is a feat of association." [40] Thus all thinking is metaphoric, and Frost gives the broadest epistemological relevance to metaphor in "Education by Poetry." It is not a simple "pairing-off" correspondence, which would be static; he is careful not to use the word "simile" except facetiously, as in "The Door in the Dark."

> In going from room to room in the dark
> I reached out blindly to save my face,
> But neglected, however lightly, to lace
> My fingers and close my arms in an arc.

A slim door got in past my guard,
And hit me a blow in the head so hard
I had my native simile jarred.
So people and things don't pair anymore
With what they used to pair with before.

His "native simile," adept at pairing "people and things," did not
open the door, only ran into it "in the dark." Metaphors are creative, door-opening, expansive, and the main value of teaching
poetry is that it teaches awareness of metaphor. ("Education by
poetry is education by metaphor.") It provides discipline and
direction and understanding in its function as the "prism of the
intellect" which takes "enthusiasm," the raw emotional response
to experience, and spreads it "on the screen in a color, all the way
from hyperbole at one end—or overstatement, at one end—to understatement at the other end." [41] It is thus a way of sorting out, of
discriminating, meaning from the language that contains it. It is
also a warning, as was "Maple," against the heresy of thinking that
meaning is absolute:

> Once on a time all the Greeks were busy telling each other what
> the All was—or was like unto. All was three elements, air, earth,
> and water (we once thought it was ninety elements; now we
> think it is only one). All was substance, said another. All was
> change, said a third. But best and most fruitful was Pythagoras'
> comparison of the universe with number. Number of what?
> Number of feet, pounds, and seconds was the answer, and we
> had science and all that has followed in science. The metaphor
> has held and held, breaking down only when it came to the
> spiritual and psychological or the out of the way places of the
> physical. [42]

This proper relation to meaning that one establishes through metaphor carries over into all aspects of living—into historical perspec-
tives and personal values. A proper understanding of figurative
values liberates one to the possibilities of Belief—or all four beliefs.
Yet it finally has the limitation of the finite mind:

Greatest of all attempts to say one thing in terms of another is the philosophical attempt to say matter in terms of spirit, or spirit in terms of matter, to make the final unity. That is the greatest attempt that ever failed. We stop just short there. But it is the height of poetry, the height of all thinking, the height of all poetic thinking, that attempt to say matter in terms of spirit and spirit in terms of matter. It is wrong to call anybody a materialist simply because he tries to say spirit in terms of matter, as if that were a sin. Materialism is not the attempt to say all in terms of matter. The only materialist—be he poet, teacher, scientist, politician, or statesman—is the man who gets lost in his material without a gathering metaphor to throw it into shape and order. He is the lost soul.[43]

Thus through over sixty years of writing about poetry, and through a tantalizing variety of literary forms and styles, Robert Frost has left us a body of critical theory that is probably larger than that of any other American poet. It has scope and depth, wit and subtlety—and a great sanity. In its significance, it bears favorable comparison with the formalized criticism of Eliot or Pound, yet its dependence on Emerson gives it a more distinctive American quality. Finally, it should be remembered that Frost told John Freeman: "my theory was out of my practice"; he exemplified its relevance in the poetry he wrote.

FROST AS A PRACTICAL CRITIC

"Each poem clarifies something. But then you've got to do it again. You can't get clarified to stay so: let you not think that. In a way, it's like nothing more than blowing smoke rings. Making little poems encourages a man to see that there is shapeliness in the world. A poem is an arrest of disorder."

Robert Frost, quoted in an interview by John Ciardi, published in the *Saturday Review*, March 21, 1959.

When we turn to Frost's practical criticism, our first impression is likely to be one of surprise at how low-keyed it is. There is, moreover, something curiously superficial about his literary judgments. Certainly this is due in part to the informality of his letter style, partly to certain difficulties in his personality, and very largely to the fact that he was not particularly interested in practical criticism. In looking at this aspect of Frost's literary mind, we are limited by the available evidence. Not all his letters have been published and almost none of his lectures, which would seem to be an important primary source. Any assessment, therefore, will have to change, as new material becomes public. But in the material that is at present available, Frost's criticism covers three distinct areas: judgments about his own poetry, about the poetry of his contemporaries, and about the poetry of the past.

Unfortunately there is far too little record of Frost's comments on his own poetry. His criticism here is restricted mostly to his early work, and is almost wholly concerned with technique. The same diffidence that kept him from commenting on his major contemporaries also kept him out of controversy over his own poetry. "I have written to keep the over curious out of the secret places of my mind both in my verse and in my letters to such as you," he wrote to Sidney Cox.[1] Or perhaps the reason for a lack of self-analysis was simply that, since a poem had been an act of clarification for him, it did not bear further clarification; he was usually sure about what he had written. There is barely restrained impatience in the tone of his letter to Leonidas W. Payne Jr., chairman of the English Department at the University of Texas, when Payne, with misguided good will, sent Frost a list of "errors" found in his *Collected Poems*. (Page 105) There is no room for self-doubt here; he was not to be misled by standards of "school-girl English."

Most of Frost's self-criticism, probably because it deals with the early poetry, is directed at his major preoccupations at that time—sound, and tones of voice. In a conversation with Louis Mertins, he talks of the problem of diction:

When I first began to write poetry—before the illumination of what possibilities there are in the sound of sense came to me—I was writing largely, though not exclusively, after the pattern of the past. For every poet begins that way—following some pattern, or group of patterns. It is only when he has outgrown the pattern, and sees clearly for himself his own way that he has really started to become. You may go back to all those early poems of mine in *A Boy's Will*, and some that are left out of it. You will find me there using the traditional clichés. Even "Into My Own" has an "as't were." In "Stars" there is a line "O'er the tumultuous snow"; while in my very first poem "My Butterfly," I was even guilty of "theeing" and "thouing," a crime I have not committed since.[2] *

But this is mostly hindsight. He expresses less consciousness of words as clichés, and more concern for the relation of sound to logic in the following 1894 letter to Susan Hayes Ward about the first poem ("My Butterfly") that she accepted for *The Independent*:

I have not succeeded in revising the poem as you requested. That Aztec consonant syllable of mine, "l," spoils a word I am very sorry to dispense with. The only one I think of to substitute for it is "eddying" which of course weakens the impression—although I am not sure but that it merely changes it. The would-be cadence howe'er may be incorrect also, but I did not suspect it at the time. It is used in the same sense as "at any rate" would be in that case. But I cannot sustain the usage by any example I have in mind: and when once I doubt an idiom my ear hesitates to vouch for it thereafter. The line, "These were the unlearned things," is wretched. It refers directly to the two lines preceeding and indirectly to the answer inevitable to that question "And did you think etc." which answer would be, God did nevertheless! Yet the line is manifestly redundant as well as retruse and I must invent one to supplant it.[3]

This concern for the relation of sound to sense is even more evident in his criticism of slightly later poems, which more directly embody his theories of intonation. His analysis of the value of "A Patch of Snow," for example, is based on the dual criteria of

* From *Robert Frost: Life and Talks-Walking*, by Louis Mertins. Copyright © 1965 by the University of Oklahoma Press.

"certain points of recognition" and "the very special tone." (Page 64) And one of his fullest criticisms of his own poetry, in his own critical terms, occurs in an unpublished lecture (Page 143) that he gave to the Browne and Nichols School in 1915; his "terms" are wholly those of intonation:

> . . . the Sound in the mouths of men I found to be the basis of all effective expression,—not merely words or phrases, but sentences,—living things flying round,—the vital parts of speech. And my poems are to be read in the appreciative tones of this live speech. For example, there are five tones in this first stanza,

"The Pasture"

I'm going out to clean the pasture spring;	(light, informing tone)
I'll only stop to rake the leaves away	("only" tone—reservation)
(And wait to watch the water clear, I may):	(supplementary, possibility)
I sha'n't be gone long.—You come too.	(free tone, assuring)
	(afterthought, inviting)
I'm going out to fetch the little calf	(similar, free, persuasive, assur-
That's standing by the mother. It's so young,	suasive, assur-
It totters when she licks it with her tongue.	ing, and invit-
I sha'n't be gone long.—You come too.	ing tones in second stanza)

Yet if intonation is the chief criterion in Frost's self-criticism, it rests on a thorough knowledge of metrics. In a letter to John Erskine, he reads lines in terms of their meter, and admits to having a "sophisticated ear." (Page 98) There is, moreover, a critical judgment at work in the very ordering of the poems in *A Boy's Will*, and especially in the rubrics that accompanied the poems in the first edition. There is an element of self-parody, of irony, of critical objectivity, and an awareness of over-all structure in this random selection from the original table of contents:

INTO MY OWN *The youth is persuaded that he will be rather more than less himself for having forsworn the world.*

MY NOVEMBER GUEST *He is in love with being misunderstood.*

IN NEGLECT *He is scornful of folk his scorn cannot reach.*

MOWING *He takes up life simply with the small tasks.*

REVELATION *He resolves to become intelligible, at least to himself, since there's no help else.*

NOW CLOSE THE WINDOWS *It is time to make an end of speaking.*

MY BUTTERFLY *There are things that can never be the same.*

The rubrics in fact shift the "voice" in each poem from that of adolescent romanticism close to that of the ironic monologues of the early Eliot. It seems a pity they were removed from later editions, though they are restored in the notes of the 1969 edition by Edward Connery Lathem. Perhaps Frost thought they were too obvious, or perhaps he came to think that the "voice" had to validate itself from *within* the poem.

On the whole, although Frost's judgments about his own poetry were very sure, he rarely indulged in self-justification. About "The Road Not Taken," for example, which he knew was being misread by most readers, he remained enigmatically noncommital. Commenting on the preference of Maine publisher Thomas Mosher for "Reluctance," Frost notes: "Nevertheless the book contains a dozen poems that are at least good in the same kind and for the same reason. In Mowing, for instance, I come so near what I long to get that I almost despair of coming nearer." [4] "Mowing" is indeed the one poem in *A Boy's Will* that stands out as something stronger than a Romantic lyric, and that prefigures the best of Frost's poetry; one would love to hear him analyze what it was he came so close to "getting," as Poe analyzed the composition of "The Raven." But Frost gives little away.

The bulk of his criticism is directed rather toward his contemporaries, and the criteria he employs here are only slightly broader than those involved in his self-criticism. Again, although the time span is larger, his primary emphasis is on technique and craftsmanship. His praise goes to any demonstration of technical mastery, as in his comment on Mark Van Doren's "Winter Diary": "I believe I saw how you got every turn of phrase and word-shift in it. I de-

lighted in the way you took your rhymes." [5] His praise goes also
to any work that illustrates his own theories, as the "speaking tones"
do in Edwin Arlington Robinson's *The Porcupine*. (Page 94) His
condemnation goes to anything that runs counter to his practical
knowledge of the way poetry works. Thus he is skeptical of
Bridges' syllabic theory of metrics. In a marginal comment beside
a poem of Bridges' in the 1913 issue of *Poetry and Drama*, Frost
writes:

> I heard this great man in a brave theory of rhythm at lunch at
> the Vienna Cafe not long since. He holds that our syllables are to
> be treated in verse as having quantities of many shades. That is to
> say they are quarter, third and fifth notes as the case may be.
> Who knows not that, nor acts upon it, is no poet. Well here
> we have him acting upon it, we are to presume. Poor old man.[6]

Yet even here Frost has enough tolerance to admit: "Mind you he
has done good things." He is more scathing toward sheer incompetence. Note his emphasis on structure, as well as on "recognition,"
in this comment on Wilfred Gibson's "Solway Ford":

> It is a good poem. But it is oh terribly made up. You know very
> well that at most all he had to go on was some tale he had heard
> of a man who had gone mad from fear and another of a man
> who had been pinned and overtaken by the tide in Solway. I
> am even inclined to think he invented the latter. It hardly sounds
> plausible. The details of what he asks you to believe his hallu-
> cinations were are poetical but not very convincing. And then
> look at the way the sentences run on. They are not sentences at
> all in my sense of the word.[7]

Although the tone of a letter Frost wrote to Harold Monro about
Monro's poetry is jocular and tactful, he plainly cannot bring himself to accept exaggerated diction: "You turn life rather too terrible
by the use of such words over a cat drinking milk as 'creeping lust,'
'transfigured with love,' 'dim ecstasy,' 'her world is an infinite shapeless white,' 'holy drop,' and 'lies defeated.'" [8]

Gibson and Monro were friends of Frost. The tone is less tactful and the attack on technical incompetence more direct and specific in his letters on Clement Wood and James Agee. (Pages 96 and 109) Frost insists on traditional grammar and logic in his criticism of Agee's poem. Delicacy of tone could never cover up sloppiness in thinking; form must lead to clarification, or it belies itself.

This emphasis on technique as a critical yardstick has firmness and practicality, but it excludes a great deal. Predating the New Criticism, it has some of the limitations of that approach. On the whole, it pays too little attention to the psychological and moral values that go into writing, to a writer's intention, or to his relation to his culture. Frost's critical approach thus lacks a philosophical center; he tends to get drowned in the shallows. At one extreme, this lack prevents his seeing the importance of Eliot's innovations; at the other extreme, it lets in a certain personal peevishness, as in many of his comments on Pound. The inscription that Pound wrote in a copy of *Cantos LII–LXXI* which he presented to Frost shrewdly touches on this restrictiveness: "For R.F. who w'd like it— if he w'd like it—E.P." [9]

There is a significant exception to this limitation in Frost's critical vision—enough to prove that his critical capabilities were broader than the bulk of his criticism would indicate. That exception is the preface to Robinson's *King Jasper*, one of the few pieces of formal criticism that Frost attempted. The second half of that preface is devoted to particularized analysis of individual poems; but the second half was an appendage, added only after the publisher asked Frost for a few more pages. Frost's essential approach to Robinson is through the latter's subject matter—his "griefs," "Robinsonianly profound"—and through his "style," the inner toughness by which he prevented his griefs from becoming mere yelping grievances. Frost reveals a touching sensitivity to Robinson's lost aching spirit, and a generosity that, through a "recognition" that is more literary than biographical, allows him to identify with it. It is a sound humanistic piece of criticism that enters fully into the spirit of its subject.

Frost rarely brought this sense of wholeness to his critical judgments. His best qualities as a critic exist on a level below this, and

they illustrate his astuteness rather than his profundity. His criticism
springs from a commitment to a definite attitude; it has discrimination, particularity, and range.

If commitment to a well-defined attitude carries with it the danger, in Frost, of leading to criticism that is simply opinionated and
often wrongheaded, it also has the balancing virtue of letting us
know where he stands. He had opinions on most of his contemporaries, and he aired them forcefully. "I always hold that we get
forward as much by hating as by loving," [10] he once noted, and
many of his critical judgments are simply concerned with separat-
ing sheep from goats. He is impatient, for example, with Untermeyer's critical pussyfooting:

> Anybody can tell you are cunning by the way you phrase your-
> self on the subject of Braithwaite's five best poems. The selection
> "staggers you." That is to say you don't say it is not good and
> you won't say you don't know what good is. You seem to allow
> that the poems have merit, though you don't see it. They have
> none.[11]

Such definiteness only becomes a critical merit by virtue of the
fact that Frost usually reveals a fine sense of discrimination in his
judgments. Certainly, there are some alarming lapses in his critical
insight. His assessment of Pound is obscured by a personal antagonism toward him. He casts Wallace Stevens off as "bric-a-brac." [12]
His judgments on Eliot—even when one makes allowances for the
facetiousness of casual expression—are fatuous:

> [Eliot] is a pessimistic Christian; I am an optimistic pagan.[13]
> I play euchre. [Eliot] plays Eucharist. We both play.[14]

Or simply whimsical:

> Such news reaches me from the great world as that common
> sense is now considered plebean and any sense at all only less
> so: the aristocrat will spurn both this season; one American
> poet living in England has made an Anthology of the Best Lines
> in Poetry. He has run the lines loosely together in a sort of nar-
> rative and copyrighted them so that anyone using them again

will have to enclose them in double quotation marks thus: " 'I say no harm and I mean no harm.' " [15]

Such oversimplification is particularly disappointing when one considers how close some of Frost's theories about art are to those explored in *Four Quartets*. Perhaps the most puzzling limitation of all is his apparent neglect of the later Yeats; there seems to be no mention of Yeats in Frost's criticism after 1915. Nevertheless, despite these major lapses, Frost's judgments of contemporary sheep and goats reveal a sharp discrimination. He senses that Masters, with all his "false realism," and Sandburg, with his affectations and post-Whitman effusions, are minor figures. Amy Lowell is little better, though she is saved somewhat by her Brahmin rigor. But he responds with generous conviction to the stronger talents of Robinson, Edward Thomas, D. H. Lawrence, Hardy, and the early Yeats. His response to D. H. Lawrence is typical. At the end of a letter to Edward Garnett he writes: "I'll tell you a poet with a method that is a method: Lawrence. I came across a poem of his in a new Imagiste Anthology just published here, and it was such a poem that I wanted to go right to the man that wrote it and say something." [16] And at a time when contemporary judgment was unbelievably confusing the talents of Alfred Noyes and W. B. Yeats, Frost wrote a shrewd clarification of their respective merits (Page 89). Living in the midst of the English Georgians, he could distinguish their relative value:

The nineties produced no single poem to put beside [De la Mare's] "Listeners." Really the nineties had very little on these degenerate days when you consider. Yeats, Jonson [Lionel Johnson] and Dowson they had, and that is about all. De la Mare and Davies are the equal of any of them in lyric and Abercrombie . . . leaves them all behind in the sublime imaginative sort of thing. [17]

The same sense of generous and sane discrimination is revealed in Frost's comments on the individual poems in the *Miscellany of American Poetry* (Page 100), or in the Preface to *The Arts Anthology: Dartmouth Verse 1925* (Page 116).

In several of his letters and conversations Frost creates the image of a reader who runs his finger down a page of a poem and notes, at a certain line, "There you've hit it." The image could perhaps be taken as a paradigm of Frost's critical method, for the quality of particularity thus illustrated was one of its strongest points. Such particularity has some relation, as Frost himself noted, to Poe's idea that poetic excellence comes in short bursts, that in a long poem the high points are necessarily strung together by patches of mediocrity. But it does suggest, also, that both careful reading and sharp judgment go into Frost's critical statements, for he was fond of singling out particular lines. "You never wrote better lines than the last three in The Innkeeper," he wrote John Erskine.[18] In a tactful criticism of a poem by his son Carol (Page 107), after commenting on its subject matter and general approach, he singles out particular lines:

> How I like the smooth clarity and high sentiment of
>   "The place for me"
>   "And me"
>
> and from there on a way. I think the best of all may be the passage
>
>   "replenished clear
> And cold from mountain streams that ever hear
> Proceeding waters calling from below."

And in a breezy series of snap judgments on the "best" poems of various contributors to Untermeyer's 1925 *Miscellany of American Poetry*, he is careful to comment on single lines:

> The best Aiken poem is probably Arachne, . . . the best HD the Recording Angel . . . the best Eliot I or II or possibly III, the best Fletcher To Hell with Whores (line 21), . . . the best Vachel Buffaloes, . . . the best Edna Saint I (the rest are pretty bad except for line 8 in V and stanza 2 in VII).[19]

One of the most marked characteristics of Frost's practical criticism is its range. It embraces the poetry of students (*e.g.*, his preface to the Dartmouth anthology), of family (all his children wrote poems), of personal friends like Untermeyer or John Erskine or Mark Van Doren. In discussing such poetry Frost reveals tact, constructiveness, discrimination, and a tolerance for poetic attitudes not his own. To one student, for example, he writes:

> The book has come and I have read your poems first. They are good. They have loveliness—they surely have that. They are carried high. What you long for is in them. You wish the world better than it is, more poetical. You are that kind of poet. I would rate as the other kind. . . . We can be friends across the difference.[20]

Beyond the work of immediate friends, Frost's criticism embraces most of the poetic schools of the 1910's and 1920's, such as the Imagists and the *Vers-Librists*, though here he was more objective and antagonistic. Although he did not automatically classify and condemn individual members of these schools ("Fletcher is a whole lot better than I expected him to be. I have mixed him up too much with Amy to be fair to him"), yet he was opposed to "schools" in general, and to these two in particular. His main quarrel with the Imagists was that they concentrated too much on the visual imagination, consequently neglecting the essential "vocal imagination," and that their poetry was too cerebral. Sending a copy of *Mountain Interval* to Edward Garnett, Frost commented:

> I can hear Edward Thomas saying in defense of In the Home Stretch that it would cut just as it is into a dozen or more of your Chinese impressionistic poems and perhaps gain something by the cutting for the reader whose taste had been formed on the kiln-dried tabule poetry of your Pounds and Masterses. I look on theirs as synthetical chemical products put together after a formula. It's too long a story to go into with anyone I'm not sure it wouldn't bore. There's something in the living sentence (in the shape of it) that is more important than any phrasing or chosen word. And it's something you can only achieve when going free. The Hill Wife ought to be some sort of answer to you.[21]

With the "free-versters," as he called them, his quarrel was deeper, since he regarded form as a philosophical as well as a technical necessity. Since the basic discipline of straining the meter against the rhythm was not required, free verse, he claimed, could be written by any fool. In a letter to Leonidas W. Payne Jr., commenting on the slowness of Texas trains, Frost tosses off his own parody:

> And yet speed is a thing I can see the beauty of and intend to write a poem in free verse on if ever I am tempted to write anything in free verse. Let's see how do you write the stuff:
>
> > Oh thou that spinnest the wheel
> > Give speed
> > Give such speed
> > That in going from point A
> > To point B
> > I may not have had time to forget A
> > Before I arrive at B
> > And there may result comparison
> > And metaphor
> > From the presence in the mind
> > Of two images at the same instant practically.[22]

A more bitter parody was the free-verse letter Frost wrote to Pound, but never sent. (Page 87)

A "school" or rather a literary attitude that became increasingly popular during the 1920's and 1930's was one that sought to bring literature to the service of politics. Frost was equally disdainful of this. To Archibald MacLeish's view that originality in art can precipitate revolution in politics, Frost's rebuttal was characteristically pragmatic:

> Tell me any poetic or belle lettre originality of any day that became the revolution of any day following. Let's talk sense. Wordsworth and Emerson both wrote some politics into their verse. Their poetic originality by which they live was quite another thing. So of Shelley. His originality was sufficient to

give him his place. His politics were of the order of Godwins and Orages. If you want to play with the word revolution, every day and every new poem of a poet is a revolution of the spirit: that is to say it is a freshening. But it leads to nothing on the lower plane of politics. On the lower plane of thought and opinion the poet is a follower. Generally he keeps pretty well off that plane for that reason.[23]

Disdaining such "grievances" in favor of "griefs" as material for poetry, Frost stayed clear of propagandist verse. He could no more write for a specific cause than he could write for a specific occasion. The poem he actually wrote for President Kennedy's inauguration was little better than doggerel, and there is a strong suspicion current among Frost's friends that the inability to read this poem and the on-the-spot substitution of "The Gift Outright" was a well-calculated piece of acting. Yet Frost was always interested in politics and more than one of his poems can be read in political terms. Although he was chary of having "Mending Wall" interpreted as a confrontation of a nationalist and an internationalist point of view, and although he openly denied that "To a Thinker in Office" dealt with President Roosevelt, yet he himself offers a "political" reading of "The Death of the Hired Man" in his *Paris Review* interview:

They think I'm no New Dealer. But really and truly I'm not, you know, all that clear on it. In *The Death of the Hired Man* that I wrote long, long ago, long before the New Deal, I put it two ways about home. One would be the manly way: "Home is the place where, when you have to go there, They have to take you in." That's the man's feeling about it. And then the wife says, "I should have called it/ Something you somehow hadn't to deserve." That's the New Deal, the feminine way of it, the mother way. You don't have to deserve your mother's love. You have to deserve your father's. He's more particular. One's a Republican, one's a Democrat. The father is always a Republican toward his son, and his mother's always a Democrat. Very few have noticed that second thing; they've always noticed the sarcasm, the hardness of the male one.[24]

Besides Edwin Arlington Robinson, the two contemporaries to whom Frost gave greatest critical attention were Edward Thomas and Amy Lowell. Though he wrote no formal tribute to Thomas' poetry, as he did to Robinson's, his "criticism" lay in urging Thomas to give up prose and cultivate the distinctive poetic quality of his mind. The story of their friendship is a moving one. Of all the poets he met in England, Thomas was his only soul mate, "the only brother I ever had," and they were bound as much by their temperamental melancholy as by their love of nature. Thomas had been grinding out a living writing hack prose. Frost started him on poetry, and, after Thomas' death, helped to spread the appreciation of his work. Frost sets out the role he played in an unpublished letter to Ben Miller:

Dear Mr. Miller:

Of course I am pleased to have Edward Thomas' name connected with mine, as I think he would be; one has to be careful to put it just the right way. I didn't show him how to write. All I did was show him himself in what he had already written. I made him see that much of his prose is poetry, that only had to declare itself in form to win him a place where he belonged among the poets. Van Doren comes near enough to the facts of our relationship and he is absolutely perfect in his description of Thomas' kind of poetry. J. C. Squire (Editor of Mercury) said to me the other day he thought Thomas the best of recent British poets. I am glad it has come to that. . . .

                                   Always yours faithfully,
                                   Robert Frost [25]

Toward Amy Lowell, his attitude is far more ambivalent. He comes to her not by way of friendship (as with Thomas), nor by way of similar poetic theories and values (as with Robinson), but by way of a curious mixture of rivalry and condescension. When he arrived back in America, after his years in England, the first review of his work that he saw was one by Amy Lowell in the *New Republic*. A few days later he called on her in Boston, where her social and poetic prominence were awesome. From an initial dependence, his attitude to her went through many phases. A letter to her in 1915 (Page 95) is a careful blend of conciliation (". . . I liked your book when I was a free agent"), reservation ("I wish sometimes you would leave to Browning some of the broader intonations . . ."), and conspiratorial chumminess ("We have busted 'em up as with cavalry. We have, we have we have"). Clearly, his critical standpoint here is ambivalent. The same mixture of dependence and independence is present in a letter in 1917, shortly after Miss Lowell had devoted to Frost a chapter in her *Tendencies in Modern American Poetry.* "Your generosity from the first has had so much to do with making me," he wrote to her, "that if from now on you reversed yourself and tried to unmake me, I should never be brought to believe you were anything but my friend." Yet there is a testiness in the way he corrects some of her "errors of fact":

Please spell it *Elinor* Frost in the two places where you name my wife. The word should be "shock" instead of "shook" in the quotation from A Hundred Collars. . . . Even if you don't care to bother with the correction in your next edition, I wish you would make a marginal note of the fact that I didn't meet Gibson till I was putting the last touches on North of Boston and I didn't meet Abercrombie till after the MS was in David Nutt's hands.[26]

A couple of weeks later, Frost wrote to Untermeyer about the same book, giving him "one or two facts that Amy leaves out of my account," and the testiness is more evident. One assertion in her book that justifiably rankled with Frost was that he lacked a sense of humor:

I doubt if she is right in making me so grim, not to say morbid. I may not be funny enough for Life or Punch, but I have sense of humor enough, I must believe, to laugh when the joke is on me as it is in some of this book of Amy's.

I really like least her mistake about Elinor. That's an unpardonable attempt to do her as the conventional helpmeet of genius. . . . What a cheap common unindividualized picture Amy makes of her.[27]

Yet the awe and a tentative liking are still there too: "Amy means well and perhaps you will come to our rescue without coming in conflict with Amy or contradicting her to her face."

By 1920, both the awe and the liking had disappeared, and Frost's independence asserts itself emphatically:

> But I'll whisper you something that by and by I mean to say above a whisper: I have about decided to throw off the light mask I wear in public when Amy is the theme of conversation. I don't believe she is anything but a fake, and I refuse longer to let her wealth, social position, and the influence she has been able to purchase and cozen, keep me from honestly bawling her out— that is, when I am called on to speak! I shan't go out of my way to deal with her yet awhile, though before all is done I shouldn't wonder if I tried my hand at exposing her for a fool as well as fraud. Think of saying that as the French have based their free verse on Alexandrines so she has based her polyphonic prose on the rhythms of the periodic sentence of oratory. She couldn't get away with that if she hadn't us all corralled by her wealth and social position. What could "periodic" have to do with it. Periodic sentences have no particular rhythm. Periodic sentences are sentences in which the interest is suspended as in a plot story. Nonsense and charlatanry—that's all that kind of talk amounts to. I'm sure she guessed without looking it up that there must be something recurrent like beat or pulse implied in periodic. She knew ladies were periodic because they recurred monthly. She's loony—and so periodic by the moon herself. Feeling as I do you don't think it would be honester for me to refuse to be bound between the covers of the same book with her, do you? [28]

In April 1925, Miss Lowell gave a gala party in Boston to launch her badly reviewed Keats biography. Frost and Untermeyer declined to go to what Frost called her "Keats Eats." Yet it is a mark of Frost's maturity and critical perspective that when she died a month later he refused to let any feelings of guilt sentimentalize his judgment:

I didn't rise to verse, but I did write a little compunctious prose to her ashes. And I did go before the assembled college to say in effect that really no one minded her outrageousness because it never thrust home: in life she didn't know where the feelings were to hurt them, any more than in poetry she knew where they were to touch them. I refused to weaken abjectly.[29]

The "little compunctious prose" was a review published in *The Christian Science Monitor* (Page 136), and it reveals some of Frost's best critical qualities—not the warm insights of identification that he gave to Robinson, but tact, positiveness, and careful discrimination. And if we can read his reservations between the lines, the review nevertheless provides a genuine clarification of her poetic value, and an acknowledgment that poetry, like religion, has many varieties of experience.

Finally, there is the criticism that Frost directs at earlier poets. This is small in bulk and, except for two essays on Emerson, even more casually indicated than his other practical criticism. But it is important as showing the range and selectivity of his reading, and—if "criticism" can include a simple declaration of what one likes—the direction of his poetic preferences.

In English poetry, he frequently quoted Chaucer and Shakespeare for the virility of their language, and the force of their speaking tones.[30] Wordsworth he liked for his attempt to get back to a speaking diction (indeed the ideas expressed in the Preface to the *Lyrical Ballads* have much in common with Frost's own theories) as well as for his appreciation of the natural world.[31] He admired Browning for the "intonations" of his dramatic monologues. When Frost's daughter Marjorie died, it was Arnold's Cadmus and Harmonia with which he plaintively identified. He read widely in English poetry, and, if much of his reading was through Palgrave's *Golden Treasury*, the battered state of his personal volumes of Wordsworth, Browning, and Arnold carry at least some evidence of more extended enthusiasms.[32]

He read even more widely, and directed more critical attention, to his American heritage, and not only to its poetry. Throughout his life he extolled Twain's "Jumping Frog" for capturing vernacular rhythms. He paid tribute to William Dean Howells: "My obligation to him . . . is not for the particular things he did in verse form, but for the perennial poetry of all his writing in all forms. I learned from him a long time ago that the loveliest theme of poetry was the voices of people." [33] His comment on the early style of Melville is perceptive: "He tried to be elegant without having first got sophisticated." [34] And he speaks with enthusiasm of the chiseled, Flaubertian prose of Willa Cather ("I wept for the sheer perfection" [35]). In poetry he admired Longfellow enough to pay him the tribute of his first book title ("Longfellow was a true poet for anyone with the ears to judge poetry by ear" [36]). Whitman he held in some suspicion, as much for his spurious ideas about democracy and the unity of man, as for his freedom with form. In the letter to Untermeyer on style (Page 78), he makes a comparative assessment of certain nineteenth-century poets:

> Emerson had one of the noblest least egotistical of styles. By comparison with it Thoreau's was conceited, Whitman's bumptious. . . . Longfellow took himself with the gentlest twinkle. . . . Whittier, when he shows any style at all, is probably a greater person than Longfellow as he is lifted priestlike above consideration of the scornful.

But the three American poets who were the most important to him were Emily Dickinson, Thoreau, and Emerson. Emily Dickinson was "the best of all women poets who ever wrote." [37] If, to a feminist, this seems backhanded praise, there is some compensation in the biographical evidence that one of his first gifts to Elinor, when they were both in high school, was a book of Emily Dickinson's poems, and in the bibliographical evidence of his own much-used copy of her poetry, which is filled with short pencil marks beside favorite poems.[38] One wishes that Frost had been more of a scribbler in margins. The full examination of his debt to her—and it would include her creation of a dramatic situation in a poem, as well as her rhythms—has yet to be made. *Walden* also remained one of his favorite books, partly for the same reason that *Robinson Crusoe* was ("I never tire of being shown how the limited can make snug in the limitless" [39]), but partly for its unversified poetry.

Frost would have agreed with Thoreau that "a true account of the actual is the rarest poetry"; and he gave the greatest possible extension of meaning to the "actual":

> I'm sure Im glad of all the unversified poetry of Walden—and not merely nature-descriptive, but narrative as in the chapter on the play with the loon on the lake, and character-descriptive as in the beautiful passage about the French-Canadian woodchopper. That last alone with some things in Turgenieff must have had a good deal to do with the making of me.[40]

But it was Emerson who remained Frost's great mentor, and Emerson who earned his most ungrudging and respectful praise. Enough has been written about Frost's philosophical relation to Emerson, and the difference in their attitudes toward the physical world.[41] Here we are concerned only with Frost's literary appraisal of him, which occurs in a review, "The Prerequisites," originally published in the *New York Times* in 1954, and an address "On Emerson," first delivered to the American Academy of Arts and Sciences in 1959.

"The Prerequisites" (Page 137) is a cryptic analysis of Emerson's poem "Brahma," and reveals some important aspects of Frost's critical method: the need, in appreciating a poem, to wait until experience has caught up with intellectual understanding; the stress on "meaning," yet with a careful differentiation between "meaning" and "information"; the importance given to "recognition"; the lack of any mention of technique; and that enigmatic final sentence: "He was a confirmed symbolist." What, then, *are* the "prerequisites"? The ability to live in a state of "negative capability" with a poem, waiting until it works its effects? The capacity for "recognition"? Simple humility, perhaps emphasized by the fairy-tale quality of the prose?

One is reminded of the image of the waterspout in which Frost had discussed poetry nearly thirty years earlier, in his preface to the Dartmouth anthology (Page 116). The point of view there was that of the poet who, in the act of creation, carries something up from the water around him ("all the life he ever lived outside of books") and something down from the cloud above ("all the other poets he ever read"). The point of view here is that of the reader, but the analogy holds; poet and reader are united, after all, by the moment of "recognition." Whatever the "prerequisites" are, Frost comes to the poem from within it and grows with it; and in the process he genuinely elucidates it and pays tribute to its value.

In the address "On Emerson," Frost acknowledges two debts to him. The first relates to Emerson's philosophical ideas, especially his ideas about freedom ("freedom is nothing but departure"). For both poets the word is far more than a political cliché; yet for both, too, the American political heritage lies behind the individual concept of freedom. Unlike many later critics, Frost is willing to be tolerant of Emerson's monism, his cheerful ignoring of evil: "A melancholy dualism is the only soundness. The question is: is soundness of the essence"? Certainly it is hardly "of the essence" in Frost's greater debt to Emerson—his literary debt. "Some of my first thinking about my own language was certainly Emersonian," he writes. And he goes on to quote the lines from "Monadnoc" that he quoted many times and in many places as being the source of his theories on diction and speech intonation:

> Yet wouldst thou learn our ancient speech
> These the masters that can teach.
> Fourscore or a hundred words
> All their vocal muse affords.
> Yet they turn them in a fashion
> Past the statesmen's art and passion.
> Rude poets of the tavern hearth
> Squandering your unquoted mirth,
> That keeps the ground and never soars,
> While Jake retorts and Reuben roars.
> Scoff of yeoman, strong and stark,
> Goes like bullet to the mark;
> And the solid curse and jeer
> Never balk the waiting ear.

These lines, he notes, "came pretty near making me an anti-vocabularian." Yet they anchor Frost securely to the American colloquial tradition.

On the whole, Frost's practical criticism is of more limited value than his critical theories. Even when gathered in one place, his practical criticism is too scattered, too casual, often too personal, and has too many lapses in judgment. It does justice to wide and comparative reading rather than to a single attitude toward literature. At its best, however, it has sophistication and wit, and gives an increased awareness that behind Frost's sense of "locality" and "colloquiality" lies a solid knowledge of the great tradition of English poetry.

Part II
The Texts

Letters

TO JOHN T. BARTLETT

John T. Bartlett (1892–1947) was a student of Robert Frost's at Pinkerton Academy from 1907 to 1909, and remained a close friend throughout his life. Shortly after graduating from Pinkerton, Bartlett went west, to work as a journalist in Vancouver. This letter was written to him there, while Frost was in England. It is one of Frost's first attempts to formalize in writing the ideas on the "sound of sense" and its interdependence with meter which had preoccupied him since the 1890's.

Fourth of July [1913] Beaconsfield

Dear John:—

Those initials you quote from T.P.'s belong to a fellow named Buckley and the explanation of Buckley is this that he has recently issued a book with David Nutt, but at his own expense, whereas in my case David Nutt assumed the risks. *And* those other people Buckley reviewed are his personal friends or friends of his friends or if not that simply examples of the kind of wrong horse most fools put their money on. You will be sorry to hear me say so but they are not even craftsmen. Of course there are two ways of using that word the good and the bad one. To be on the safe side it is best to call such dubs mechanics. To be perfectly frank with you I am one of the most notable craftsmen of my time. That will transpire presently. I am possibly the only person going who works on any but a worn out theory (principle I had better say) of versification. You see the great successes in recent poetry have been made on the assumption that the music of words was a matter of harmonised vowels and consonants. Both Swinburne and Tennyson arrived largely at effects in assonation. But they were on the wrong track or at any rate on a short track. They went the length of it. Any one else who goes that way must go after them. And that's where most are going. I alone of English writers have con-

sciously set myself to make music out of what I may call the sound
of sense. Now it is possible to have sense without the sound of
sense (as in much prose that is supposed to pass muster but makes
very dull reading) and the sound of sense without sense (as in
Alice in Wonderland which makes anything but dull reading).
The best place to get the abstract sound of sense is from voices
behind a door that cuts off the words. Ask yourself how these
sentences would sound without the words in which they are embodied:

> You mean to tell me you can't read?
> I said no such thing.
> Well read then.
> You're not my teacher.
>
> ———
>
> He says it's too late.
> Oh, say!
> Damn an Ingersoll watch anyway.
>
> ———
>
> One-two-three—go!
> No good! Come back——come back.
> Haslam go down there and make those kids get out of the
>   track.
>
> ———

Those sounds are summoned by the audile [audial] imagination
and they must be positive, strong, and definitely and unmistakeably
indicated by the context. The reader must be at no loss to give
his voice the posture proper to the sentence. The simple declara-
tive sentence used in making a plain statement is one sound. But
Lord love ye it mustn't be worked to death. It is against the law
of nature that whole poems should be written in it. If they are
written they won't be read. The sound of sense, then. You get
that. It is the abstract vitality of our speech. It is pure sound—pure
form. One who concerns himself with it more than the subject is
an artist. But remember we are still talking merely of the raw
material of poetry. An ear and an appetite for these sounds of

sense is the first qualification of a writer, be it of prose or verse. But if one is to be a poet he must learn to get cadences by skillfully breaking the sounds of sense with all their irregularity of accent across the regular beat of the metre. Verse in which there is nothing but the beat of the metre furnished by the accents of the pollysyllabic words we call doggerel. Verse is not that. Neither is it the sound of sense alone. It is a resultant from those two. There are only two or three metres that are worth anything. We depend for variety on the infinite play of accents in the sound of sense. The high possibility of emotional expression all lets in this mingling of sense-sound and word-accent. A curious thing. And all this has its bearing on your prose me boy. Never if you can help it write down a sentence in which the voice will not know how to posture *specially*.

That letter head shows how far we have come since we left Pink. Editorial correspondent of the Montreal Star sounds to me. Gad, we get little mail from you.

Affectionately   R.F.

Maybe you'll keep this discourse on the sound of sense till I can say more on it.

TO SIDNEY COX

Robert Frost and Sidney Cox (1889–1952) first met when they were both teaching in Plymouth, New Hampshire, in 1911. Despite a difference in age (Frost was thirty-seven and Cox twenty-two at the time) and an initial clash in personalities, they became firm and lifelong friends, though the roles always retained something of a devotee-and-idol quality. During his long and distinguished career as a Professor of English at Dartmouth College, Sidney Cox was one of the first persons in the United States to include Frost's work in a literature syllabus; and when he wrote his fine impressionistic biography, A Swinger of Birches, Frost, if somewhat grudgingly, paid Cox the rare tribute of writing the Preface to it. Perhaps because Cox was such a dedicated teacher, many of Frost's letters to him about his poetic theories are not only explicatory and analytical but also carry a tone of professional assurance.

19 January 1914 Beaconsfield

Dear Cox

Absolve me of trying to make you think of me as hobnobbing with the great over here and I am ready to begin my *very* short talks based on Quiller-Couch. I'm far from important enough for the likes of the Poet Laureate to have sought me out. I'm simply going to tell you about him because I happen to have eaten at the same table with him by an accident. I was visiting Lawrence Binyon (see anthology) when Bridges turned up. I have a right to tell you how the king looked to the cat that looked at him.

He's a fine old boy with the highest opinion—of his poetry you thought I was going to say—perhaps of his poetry, but much more particularly of his opinions. He rides two hobbies tandem, his theory that syllables in English have fixed quantity that cannot be disregarded in reading verse, and his theory that with forty or fifty or sixty characters he can capture and hold for all time the sounds of speech. One theory is as bad as the other and I think owing to much the same fallacy. The living part of a poem is the intonation entangled somehow in the syntax idiom and meaning of a sentence. It is only there for those who have heard it previously in conversation. It is not for us in any Greek or Latin poem because our ears have not been filled with the tones of Greek and Roman talk. It is the most volatile and at the same time important part of poetry. It goes and the language becomes a dead language, the poetry dead poetry. With it go the accents the stresses the delays that are not the property of vowels and syllables but that are shifted at will with the sense. Vowels have length there is no denying. But the accent of sense supercedes all other accent over-rides and sweeps it away. I will find you the word "come" vari-ously used in various passages as a whole, half, third, fourth, fifth, and sixth note. It is as long as the sense makes it. When men no longer know the intonation on which we string our words they will fall back on what I may call the absolute length of our syl-

lables which is the length we would give them in passages that
meant nothing. The psychologist can actually measure this with a
what-do-you-call-it. English poetry would then be read as Latin
poetry is now read and as of course Latin poetry was never read
by Romans. Bridges would like it read so now for the sake of
scientific exactness. Because our poetry must sometime be as dead
as our language must, Bridges would like it treated as if it were
dead already.

I say you cant read a single good sentence with the salt in it
unless you have previously heard it spoken. Neither can you with
the help of all the characters and diacritical marks pronounce a
single word unless you have previously heard it actually pronounced. Words exist in the mouth not in books. You can't fix
them and you dont want to fix them. You want them to adapt
their sounds to persons and places and times. You want them to
change and be different. I shall be sorry when everybody is so
public-schooled that nobody will dare to say Haow for What. It
pleases me to contemplate the word Sosieti that the reformers sport
on their door plate in a street in London. The two i's are bad
enough. But the o is what I love. Which o is that if we must be
exact.

Bridges wants to fix the vocables here and now because he sees
signs of their deteriorating. He thinks they exist in print for people.
He thinks they are of the eye. Foolish old man is all I say. How
much better that he should write good poetry if he hasn't passed
his time. He has been a real poet, though you never would judge
it from a thing in the Dec[ember] Poetry and Drama in which he
takes the unsentimental view of teachers that they cram us with
dead dry stuff like the dead flies on the window sill.

You will have to import your own books I'm afraid, unless
Sherman French & Co of Boston would get them for you. Books
and postage in the awful quantity you mention would cost you
four American dollars. You mustn't get one book more than you
honestly feel that you can dispose of. No silly promises are binding.

                                              Yours   R Frost

Make you a present of all the words I have misspelled in this letter.
They'll do you good if they correct a little your tendency to think
as a teacher that everything must be correct.

TO JOHN T. BARTLETT

This letter continues Frost's speculations about intonation into the field of sentence structure. It may be useful to read his comments on "A Patch of Snow" in the light of the poem as it actually emerged:

> *There's a patch of old snow in a corner,*
> *That I should have guessed*
> *Was a blow-away paper the rain*
> *Had brought to rest.*
>
> *It is speckled with grime as if*
> *Small print overspread it,*
> *The news of a day I've forgotten—*
> *If I ever read it.*

22 February 1914 Beaconsfield

Dear John:

[. . .] I want to write down here two or three cardinal principles that I wish you would think over and turn over now and again till we *can* protract talk.

I give you a new definition of a sentence:

A sentence is a sound in itself on which other sounds called words may be strung.

You may string words together without a sentence-sound to string them on just as you may tie clothes together by the sleeves and stretch them without a clothes line between two trees, but—it is bad for the clothes.

The number of words you may string on one sentence-sound is not fixed but there is always danger of over loading.

The sentence-sounds are very definite entities. (This is no literary mysticism I am preaching.) They are as definite as words. It is not impossible that they could be collected in a book though I don't at present see on what system they would be catalogued.

They are apprehended by the ear. They are gathered by the ear from the vernacular and brought into books. Many of them are already familiar to us in books. I think no writer invents them. The most original writer only catches them fresh from talk, where they grow spontaneously.

A man is all a writer if *all* his words are strung on definite recognizable sentence sounds. The voice of the imagination, the speaking voice must know certainly how to behave how to posture in every sentence he offers.

A man is a marked writer if his words are largely strung on the more striking sentence sounds.

A word about recognition: In literature it is our business to give people the thing that will make them say, "Oh yes I know what you mean." It is never to tell them something they dont know, but something they know and hadnt thought of saying. It must be something they recognize.

A Patch of Old Snow

In the corner of the wall where the bushes haven't been trimmed, there is a patch of old snow like a blow-away newspaper that has come to rest there. And it is dirty as with the print and news of a day I have forgotten, if I ever read it.

Now that is no good except for what I may call certain points of recognition in it: patch of old snow in a corner of the wall,— you know what that is. You know what a blow-away newspaper is. You know the curious dirt on old snow and last of all you know how easily you forget what you read in papers.

Now for the sentence sounds. We will look for the marked ones because they are easiest to discuss. The first sentence sound will do but it is merely ordinary and bookish: it is entirely subordinate in interest to the meaning of the words strung on it. But half the effectiveness of the second sentence is in the very special tone with which you must say—news of a day I have forgotten—if I ever read it. You must be able to say Oh yes one knows how that goes. (There is some adjective to describe the intonation or cadence, but I won't hunt for it.)

One of the least successful of the poems in my book is almost saved by a final striking sentence-sound (Asking for Roses.)

Not caring so very much *what* she supposes.

Take My November Guest. Did you know at once how we say such sentences as these when we talk?

She thinks I have no eye for these.

———

Not yesterday I learned etc.

———

But it were vain to tell her so

———

Get away from the sing-song. You must hear and recognize in the last line the sentence sound that supports. No use in telling him so.

Let's have some examples pell-mell in prose and verse because I don't want you to think I am setting up as an authority on verse alone.

My father used to say—

You're a liar!

If a hen and a half lay an egg and a half etc.

A long long time ago—

Put it there, old man! (Offering your hand)

I aint a going [to] hurt you, so you needn't be scared.

Suppose Henry Horne says something offensive to a young lady named Rita when her brother Charles is by to protect her. Can you hear the two different tones in which she says their respective names. "Henry Horne! Charles!" I can hear it better than I can say it. And by oral practice I get further and further away from it.

Never you say a thing like that to a man!

And such they are and such they will be found.

Well I swan!

Unless I'm greatly mistaken—

Hence with denial vain and coy excuse

A soldier and afraid (afeared)

Come, child, come home.

The thing for me to do is to get right out of here while I am able.

No fool like an old fool.

It is so and not otherwise that we get the variety that makes it fun to write and read. *The ear does it.* The ear is the only true writer and the only true reader. I have known people who could read without hearing the sentence sounds and they were the fastest readers. Eye readers we call them. They can get the meaning by glances. But they are bad readers because they miss the best part of what a good writer puts into his work.

Remember that the sentence sound often says more than the words. It may even as in irony convey a meaning opposite to the words.

I wouldn't be writing all this if I didn't think it the most important thing I know. I write it partly for my own benefit, to clarify my ideas for an essay or two I am going to write some fine day (not far distant.)

To judge a poem or piece of prose you go the same way to work—apply the one test—greatest test. You listen for the sentence sounds. If you find some of those not bookish, caught fresh from the mouths of people, some of them striking, all of them definite and recognizable, so recognizable that with a little trouble you can place them and even name them, you know you have found a writer. [. . .]

Affectionately   Rob

TO SIDNEY COX

Soon after the publication of A Boy's Will *in England, in 1913, Sidney Cox began a campaign, through critical articles and through his teaching, to win Frost support at home. The following letter is typical of the way Frost "feeds" information to those who will use it advantageously. His ideas here go beyond the "sound of sense" to a more conceptual awareness of language that reveals the influence of Emerson.*

December 1914 [The Gallows]

Dear Cox

I am glad you are going into it with me and one or two others. [Edward] Thomas thinks he will write a book on what my definition of the sentence means for literary criticism. If I didn't drop into poetry every time I sat down to write I should be tempted to do a book on what it means for education. It may take some time to make people see—they are so accustomed to look at the sentence as a grammatical cluster of words. The question is where to begin the assault on their prejudice. For my part I have about decided to begin by demonstrating by examples that the sentence as a sound in itself apart from the word sounds is no mere figure of speech. I shall show the sentence sound saying all that the sentence conveys with little or no help from the meaning of the words. I shall show the sentence sound opposing the sense of the words as in irony. And so till I establish the distinction between the grammatical sentence and the vital sentence. The grammatical sentence is merely accessory to the other and chiefly valuable as furnishing a clue to the other. You recognize the sentence sound in this: *You*, you—! It is so strong that if you hear it as I do you have to pronounce the two you's differently. Just so many sentence sounds belong to man as just so many vocal runs belong to one kind of bird. We come into the world with them and create none of them. What we feel as creation is only selection and grouping. We summon them from Heaven knows where under excitement with the audile [audial] imagination. And unless we are in an imaginative mood it is no use trying to make them, they will not rise. We can only write the dreary kind of grammatical prose known as professorial. Because that is to be seen at its worst in translations especially from the classics, Thomas thinks he will take up the theme apropos of somebody's scholarly translation of Horace or Catullus some day when such a book comes his way for review.

I throw all this out as it comes to me to show you where we are at present. Use anything you please. I am only too glad of your help. We will shake the old unity-emphasis-and-coherence Rhetoric to its foundations.

A word more. We value the seeing eye already. Time we said something about the hearing ear—the ear that calls up vivid sentence forms.

We write of things we see and we write in accents we hear. Thus we gather both our material and our technique with the imagination from life; and our technique becomes as much material as material itself.

All sorts of things must occur to you. Blaze away at them. But expect to have to be patient. There are a lot of completely educated people in the world and of course they will resent being asked to learn anything new.

You aren't influenced by that Beauty is Truth claptrap. In poetry and under emotion every word used is "moved" a little or much—moved from its old place, heightened, made, made new. See what Keats did to the word "alien" in the ode. But as he made it special in that place he made it his—and his only in that place. He could never have used it again with just that turn. It takes the little one horse poets to do that. I am probably the only Am poet who haven't used it after him. No if I want to deal with the word I must sink back to its common usage at Castle Garden. I want the unmade words to work with, not the familiar made ones that everybody exclaims Poetry! at. Of course the great fight of any poet is against the people who want him to write in a special language that has gradually separated from spoken language by this "making" process. His pleasure must always be to make his own words as he goes and never to depend for effect on words already made even if they be his own.

Enough of that. I dont blame your good friend. Nor do I blame the poor educated girl who thought the little book was difficult. The "contents" notes were a piece of fooling on my part. They were not necessary and not very good.

I'd like to thank specially the fellow who picked out Mowing. I guess there is no doubt that is the best poem in Book I. We all think so over here. Thank Hatch for me too. Don't forget.

And thank yourself for all you are doing for me. I need it in this game.

I should like a good talk or three with you. On the war if you choose. On anything. You are going to do a lot all round I know. Your opinions are worth listening to because you mean to put them into action—if for no other reason. But there is no other reason as important. What a man will put into effect at any cost of time money life or lives is sacred and what counts. As I get older I dont want to hear about much else. [. . .]

Yours ever   R.F.

TO LEWIS N. CHASE

This letter is interesting in its account, which Frost frequently retold, of how his poetic method became crystallized for him by the casual comment of an acquaintance that his poetry was "too near the level of talk," and by his subsequent analysis of the relation of his poetry to this "talk." Lewis N. Chase (1873–1937) was an American critic and professor of English, who wrote a critical book on Poe, entitled Poe and his Poetry, *for the* Poetry and Life Series *in 1913.*

Amherst Mass
April 29   1917

Dear Mr Chase:

There have been real troubles (sorrows even) of late to keep me from your book and from the matter you set forth in your letter. I have just been looking at the book and rereading the letter. The book is perhaps something like what you would like to make of me. Of course I should be only too happy to have you if you can find in me half a good subject. The trouble with me is that I am neither as dead as Poe nor as interesting as Poe. That is your affair, however, not mine and if you like to see what you can do with me, why let me do what I can to help you.

Should you think best to question me I wonder or is there any prospect of your coming this way for a visit and a talk? I'm rather at a loss where to begin if you are expecting me to go ahead on my own account.

The bare biographical facts are that I was born in San Francisco in 1875, I came to Massachusetts when my father died in 1885. I was educated at Dartmouth a little while and at Harvard a little while and turned my back on schools and everything else for out-and-out farming in 1900. I did rather well in school, but toward the last of my school days it seemed to go against me to feel that I had to do well. Not all of me was enlisted in what went on in classrooms and my works were always the kind that would refuse to go when you left a single one of my wheels out.

I suppose I was pretty early preoccupied with the real problem of how this-here writing was going to be done. I only felt put off the problem by what was said by teachers. They might be after something but it wasn't what I was after. There was something to get back to, something that made everything else not worth bothering with. It was in talk, I decided. Someone had complained that a little thing of mine was "too near the level of talk." I didn't see why it shouldn't be. So I resolved to go ahead and see what would happen if I went a little nearer with it. It wasn't all obstinacy. It was inspiration. In that criticism I suddenly saw something I had been on the track of ever since I had tasted success in words with a friend I used to sit late with in old high school days. Why was a friend so much more effective than a piece of paper in drawing the living sentences out of me? I thought it might come to my having to remember exactly the shape my sentences took under provocation or under social excitement. How would a piece of paper ever get the best out of me? I was afraid I hadn't imagination enough to be really literary. And I hadn't. I have just barely enough to imitate spoken sentences. I can't keep up any interest in sentences that don't SHAPE *on some speaking tone* of voice. I'm what you would call reproductive. I like best (in my poetry at least) not to set down even an idea that is of my own thinking: I like to give it as in character when I am drawing character.

Well at this rate I shall tire you before you know it. Will you ask me a little more definitely for what you want? You know I am at Amherst professing for six months. But soon I go back to my Franconia home and my writing again.

Will you tell me if you are someone I ought to have met when I was in London between 1912 and 1915? Did you know Edward Thomas?

Sincerely yours

Robert Frost

TO GEORGE H. BROWNE

George H. Browne (1857–1931) ran the Browne and Nichols School in Cambridge, Mass. When Frost returned from England in 1915, Browne persuaded him to give some talks on poetry to the boys at the School, and the two men became frequent correspondents. When Mountain Interval *appeared in 1916, they quarreled over the use of the word "interval." Browne claimed the more accurate word was "intervale." In the following letter, Frost reveals not only the conscious accuracy of his word-choice (which he wanted in any case for "its double meaning") but a chilly resentment at any suggestion of verbal vagueness. Charles P. G. Scott was a well-known geologist, whom Frost consulted on the matter.*

[18 August 1916] [Franconia]

Intervale, with its present pronunciation and meaning, arose from a mistake. It was not formed from inter- + vale; nor would that mode of formation have been used, I think, at the time and place at which the word arose. Though some formations of this apparent kind, with inter-, as it were, an adjective, equivalent to intervening, are of older date (for example, INTERSPACE) they were not really of this kind. The explanation, which is a little subtle, involves the inherent ambiguity or two-sidedness of inter, between, and similar terms. The original word was INTERVAL. This word was spelled, in the 17th century, interval, intervall, and rarely intervale; also enterval, entervall, and rarely entervale, the spelling enter- probably representing a Scottish pronunciation between short i and short e.

Apart from this point, all these spellings represented the same pronunciation, namely in-ter-val, the last syllable being pronounced like
Val for Valentine. Certain it is, that the word spelled in the 17th
century interval, intervall, or intervale, would have become, and did
become, interval in the 19th century. Its distinctive application to a
low level tract of land (originally, to one of a series of such tracts,
found at intervals by travelers or surveyors) arose in a natural way,
and there was no need to vary its pronunciation. It is my guess,
indeed, that the pronunciation now given to intervale arose as a
literary pronunciation, among persons who saw the word spelled
intervale, meaning interval, in maps and deeds. So far as the word
is in the inherited speech of the oldest inhabitants, it must be pronounced in-ter-val, and not in-ter-vale.

Dear Browne:

You might suppose this to be my own statement of my own
position. It is the way Charles P. G. Scott puts the case for interval.
My purpose in sending it is not to disqualify you as an authority, or
to persuade you of anything, but to teach you not to assume too
lightly that nobody but yourself has a reason for what he does.
While you are about it, you might profit by looking to see if you
can't find interval (so-spelled) in Emerson's Monadnoc.

All this is not to say that intervale is not a good word, though an
accident, a sophistication, and a mistake; only that interval is another
good word.

Nearly everyone would know who Charles P. G. Scott is.

So cheer up, and don't make a long-face to everyone about how
hard you have tried to educate me in the New English language
and nothing to show for your pains.

I heartily wish you were a well man.

As Ever

Robert Frost.

TO LEWIS N. CHASE

Though the tone of this letter undoubtedly indicates a "spoofing" of professional literary criticism, the "six or a dozen or more questions" do give some serious insights into Frost's own critical preoccupations: the antagonism to "formula" poetry, the concern for verse form, the open-endedness of "poetic" subjects, the interest in "vocal value," and —perhaps most interesting of all—the emphasis on "threat" in certain poems.

Franconia N.H.
July 11   1917

Dear Mr Chase:
Did I promise you something looking you straight in the eye? Are you sure I looked you straight in the eye?
Well then if I did look you straight in the eye, here are your

Six or a Dozen or More Questions

1   Which book was I trying to make help the other by my introductory "Mending Wall takes up the theme where A Tuft of Flowers in A Boys Will laid it down"?

2   What the mischief do I mean by such an impertinence?

3   Why wouldn't some of the things in North of Boston act?

4   Your reasons for considering An Old Man's Winter Night (Mountain Interval) the best thing I ever wrote.

5   I have been accused of having a creed and letting it peep through my writing. What is the creed and where do you find it?

6   Find ten lines in North of Boston that won't scan.

7   Whose is the child in The Fear?

8   Someone has said that I am a symbolist and So-and-so is a cymbalist. Who is meant by "So-and-so"?

9   *Am* I a symbolist?

10   What is the formula of Home Burial?—of The Hill Wife?

11   Was the formula preconceived?

12   What ought to be done to the author if it was preconceived?

13   Do you begin to sense my prejudices?

14   Which of the longer poems sounds the most invented?

15   Distinguish between imagination and invention.

16   What should you call the verse-form in After Apple-picking?

17   Is the general effect of North of Boston sombre?

18   Are a hundred collars lovely to contemplate? If not would they be matter for poetry?

19   Is the cage in A Servant to Servants unbeautiful?

20   Would calling these things realistic help them?

21   Point out some of the so-called practical touches in my books.

22   Where's the inconsistancy in my having railed at people who write about the moon, flowers, brooks, Pan, and suchlike time-honored material of poetry?

23   Do you find any threat in The Wood Pile?

24   How many times have you read my books through?

25   Do separate lines in North of Boston lend themselves to quotation? Pro's and con's of this.

26   Just what *is* the Road Not Taken of A Mountain Interval?

27   Do you find any threat in The Sound of Trees?

28   Look for something unsocial in A Boys Will as compared with North of Boston.

29   What poem in N. of B. comes nearest in form to the short story?

30   What comes nearest the one-act play?

31   Classify The Mountain.

32   What is the quality of such a line as "Like one who take[s] everything said as personal to himself"? (See The Wood Pile.)

33 Has the word "Warren" the same vocal value in every one of the four places where it occurs in The Death of the Hired Man?

There!

Now for the poems for public reading. I always, or almost always, begin with The Code. I am often asked to read Brown's Descent (but it is not a good poem: I sort of did it on purpose to please a few people who gave me the subject.) The Fear, The Death of the Hired Man, Mending Wall (if I ask people to take it as a puzzle and look for the Nationalist and the Internationalist in it. I'm told it contains them.) The Wood Pile. Snow (in Mountain Interval) Birches (in M. I.) and for short ones, October, Flower Gathering, The Tuft of Flowers, To the Thawing Wind, Going for Water, The Pasture, The Road Not Taken, The Telephone and A Time to Talk are apt to go well. The eight long ones I name are my stand-bys.

The first poetry I read for myself and read all to pieces (this was at fourteen) was Poe, the next E. R. Sill the next Browning (of the Dramatic Lyrics and Romances only), the next Palgrave's Treasury (I *did* read that literally to rags and tatters. This was in 1892.) the next Matthew Arnold, the next T. E. Brown (as late as —not sure of date, but say 1910.) If you can see anything any of these did to me, I cant. Some where in there I had a great time with Emerson. I don't see much meaning in it all. It comes to me that I've been fond of Virgil too. Make what you can of it. Oh and there was Keats minus Endymion! I'd like to know what I haven't liked.* I suppose I had the first copy of Francis Thompson's first poems sold in America. Even Dowson! But before all write me as one who cares most for Shakespearean and Wordsworthian sonnets.

I wonder if coming to New England from as far away as California can have had anything to do with my feeling for New England and I wonder if my having written so much about it from as far away as old England can have helped.

Aint I a good man to search myself so hard through to so little purpose?

Not as good as you, though. You are goodness itself to be so interested.

Ask me anything and I will try to answer.

Memorable night behind the houses under the great tree in the dark with you.

Always yours
Robert Frost

* Haven't cared much for Shelley and Swinburne.

TO AMY BONNER

This unpublished letter, written seventeen years after the one to Lewis Chase, picks up the same idea of the importance of "threat" to both poet and reader. The idea ties in with Frost's almost existential belief in "form" as creating meaning in the very act of moulding raw experience. Amy Bonner was a poetry reviewer for the New York Times.

South Shaftesbury Vt
June 7   1937

My dear Miss Bonner:

Thank you for both the editorial and the letter. You'll make me think I never had a more congenial class than that of last winter at the New School. I'm glad of Mr Borghum's support. If what I said about balance is true for sculpture, it is true for all the arts somehow. I suppose it amounts to this: there are no two things as important to us in life and art as being threatened and being saved. What are ideals of form for if we arent going to be made to fear for them? All our ingenuity is lavished on getting into danger legitimately so that we may be genuinely rescued.

Sincerely yours
Robert Frost

TO LOUIS UNTERMEYER

Louis Untermeyer (1885–   ) was one of the first of the critics to take up the cause of Frost's poetry when Frost returned from England in 1915. They soon became close friends—a relationship that once more bears testimony to Frost's admirable capacity for establishing loyal and enduring personal friendships. In this analysis of "style" Frost gives some perceptive judgments on earlier poets. Note the way in which his ideas on how a writer "takes himself" link up with his consciousness of establishing a "voice" for himself in his own poems.

[Amherst, Mass.
March 10, 1924]

Dear Old Louis:

Since last I saw you I have come to the conclusion that style in prose or verse is that which indicates how the writer takes himself and what he is saying. Let the sound of Stevenson go through your mind empty and you will realize that he never took himself other than as an amusement. Do the same with Swinburne and you will see that he took himself as a wonder. Many sensitive natures have plainly shown by their style that they took themselves lightly in self-defense. They are the ironists. Some fair to good writers have no style and so leave us ignorant of how they take themselves. But that is the one important thing to know: because on it depends our likes and dislikes. A novelist seems to be the only kind of writer who can make a name without a style: which is only one more reason for not bothering with the novel. I am not satisfied to let it go with the aphorism that the style is the man. The man's ideas would be some element then of his style. So would his deeds. But I would narrow the definition. His deeds are his deeds; his ideas are his ideas. His style is the way he carries himself toward his ideas and deeds. Mind you if he is down-spirited it will be all he can do to have the ideas without the carriage. The style is out of his superfluity. It is the mind skating circles round itself as it moves forward. Emerson had one of the noblest least egotistical of styles. By comparison with it Thoreau's was conceited, Whitman's bumptious. Carlyle's way of taking himself simply infuriates me. Longfellow took himself with the gentlest twinkle. I don't suppose you know his miracle play in The Golden Legend, or Birds of Killingworth, Simon Danz, or Othere.

I own any form of humor shows fear and inferiority. Irony is simply a kind of guardedness. So is a twinkle. It keeps the reader from criticism. Whittier, when he shows any style at all, is probably a greater person than Longfellow as he is lifted priestlike above consideration of the scornful. Belief is better than anything else, and it is best when rapt, above paying its respects to anybody's doubt whatsoever. At bottom the world isn't a joke. We only joke about it to avoid an issue with someone to let someone know that we know he's there with his questions: to disarm him by seeming to have heard and done justice to his side of the standing argument. Humor is the most engaging cowardice. With it myself I have been able to hold some of my enemy in play far out of gunshot. [. . .]

Affectionately
Robert

TO JOHN FREEMAN

John Freeman (1880–1929) was an English critic, poet, and insurance broker. Frost and he had mutual friends in the lawyer Jack Haines and the poet Edward Thomas. This letter would seem to refer to some article on Frost that Freeman was thinking of writing; he did in fact publish an article on him called "In the English Tradition" for a collection edited in 1928 by J. C. Squires, Contemporary American Authors. *The quotation in the opening paragraph is from Tennyson's "The Poet." The tender recollection of Jack Haines was probably sparked by an article that Haines wrote on Frost. The reference to Melville relates to the fact that in 1926 Freeman published a critical book on the novelist. The "shade" in the final paragraph is that of Edward Thomas, killed in action in 1917; Freeman wrote a moving*

*tribute "Edward Thomas: A Memoir" which appeared as a preface to
a posthumous edition of Thomas' book* The Tenth Muse.

*In reiterating some of his basic poetic theories, Frost here presents
them with a pithiness and a critical exactness that makes the letter a
valuable summary of his early ideas.*

Ann Arbor
Michigan
U.S.A.
[November 5] [1925?]

Dear Freeman:

If I wrote myself up it would have to be in verse since I write
no prose and am scared blue at any demand on me for prose. I
suppose I could do it openly in verse with perfect propriety.
Nearly every poet has paid himself tribute at least once in verse,
of course always in the third person under some such title as "The
Poet." He will say for instance:

> The poet in a golden clime was born,
> With golden stars above,
> Dowered with the hate of hate, the scorn of scorn,
> The love of love—
>   meaning himself, Alfred.

We gather from this that Alfred was pleased to be able to say he
was at once a matchless soul and a pretty good matcher, he gave
'em as good as they sent, not just tit for tat but tat for tat. Or
don't we?

Im surprised to find all these things so long afterward still
lodged in the heart of a friend. Jack Haines is one of the faithful.
I simply must get over to see him next summer before he changes
too much from the botanist who shyly scraped acquaintance with
me over flowers in the highway near Leddington one day in 1914
and once let me stand on his shoulders to pull spleenwort from a
crevice in a cliff by matchlight in the evening.

I couldnt ask anyone to state me closer. In corroboration I
might scratch on another sheet a few more things I remember

saying in the days when my theorising was strong upon me. My theory was out of my practice and was probably a provision of nature against criticism. I haven't felt the need of talking about it as much lately as I did once. I still hold to it.

Sentences may have the greatest monotony to the eye in length and structure and yet the greatest variety to the ear in the tones of voice they carry. As in Emerson.

The imagination of the ear flags first as the spirit dies down in writing. The "voices" fail you.

Some of the highlights, the most vivid imaginative passages in poetry are of the eye, but more perhaps are [of] the ear.

The vocabulary may be what you please though I like it not too literary; but the tones of voice must be caught fresh and fresh from life. Poetry is a fresh look and a fresh listen.

The actor's gift is to execute the vocal image at the mouth. The writer's is to implicate the vocal image in a sentence and fasten it printed to the page.

I ask no machine to tell me the length of a syllable. Its length with me is entirely expressional. "Oh" may be as long as prolonged agony or as short as slight surprise.

Some have proposed inventing a notation to make sure [of] the tones intended. Some have tried to help themselves with marginal adjectives. But the sentences are a notation for indicating tones of voice. A good sentence does double duty: it conveys one meaning by word and syntax [and] another by the tone of voice it indicates. In irony the tone indicated contradicts the words.

One might make a distinction between intoned poetry and intonational poetry. Of course they interpenetrate.

The brute tones of our human throat[,] that may once have been all our meaning. I suppose there is one for every feeling we shall ever feel, yes and for every thought we shall ever think. Such is the limitation of our thought.

The tones dealt in in poetry may be the broadest or again they may be the most delicate.*

Vocal reality. . . . observation of the voice.

Even in lyric the main thing is that every sentence should be come at from a different dramatic slant.

Fool psychologists treat the five sense elements in poetry as of equal weight. One of them is nearly the whole thing. The tone-of-voice element is the unbroken flow on which the others are carried along like sticks and leaves and flowers.

———

These are scraps from a lecture I once came near reading. Here's another:

All I ask is iambic. I undertake to furnish the variety in the relation of my tones to it. The crossed swords are always the same. The sword dancer varies his position between them.

What are these articles I hear Helen Thomas has been publishing about the early loves of Edward? Am I going to be kept from seeing them?

You havent given me much time. Your letter overtook me only yesterday and here it is November 5th.

No, I only taught psychology once upon a time. Yes I am as you surmise all American-Anglo-Saxon. But I am only half a Yankee. My father † was a ninth-generation Yankee. My mother was born in Scotland, a pure Scot except, I am told, for a dash of French far back.

I was brought up on Melville. My daughters live in his home town Pittsfield Mass. Dont dare to set up to like him any better than I like him.

I know whose shade I have to thank for your kindness to me. Well the world was a [dead?] place before we found it so.

You might inscribe a book to me some time.

Sincerely yours
Robert Frost

* Probably cited Magna est Veritas and The Garden to show how my theory held at different levels[,] one almost colloquial[,] another in the grand manner.
† Old Devonshire stock.

TO F. S. FLINT

F. S. Flint (1885–1960) was an English poet whom Frost met at the opening of Harold Monro's Poetry Bookshop in London, and whose friendship he cultivated and respected. For some time the friendship seemed quite intense, though it later ran into difficulty over their differing attitudes to Ezra Pound. Frost's irritation with Pound in this letter refers to a section of the review of A Boy's Will *that Pound wrote for Harriet Monroe's* Poetry: A Magazine of Verse:

> *. . . I remember Joseph Campbell telling me of meeting a man on a desolate waste of bogs, and he said to him, "It's rather dull here"; and the man said, "Faith, ye can sit on a middan and dream stars."*
>
> *And that is the essence of folk poetry with distinction between America and Ireland. And Frost's book reminds me of these things.*

This letter gives an indication of Frost's concern for variety in the total structure of his books. But it also reveals his appreciation of definiteness in any critical stance, as well as his respect for the "people" of his poetry.

The Bungalow
Beaconsfield   Bucks
July 6   1913

Dear Flint:

I am glad of your warning against monotony. I must look to my lines. You may infer from a list of my subjects how I have tried to get variety in my material. I have the following poems in something like shape for my next book:

1 The Death of the Hired Man—an elegy
2 The Hundred Collars—a comedy
3 The Black Cottage—a monologue

But variety of material will not excuse me for lack of it in treatment. I shall have to take care.

I am grateful for what I got out of you. I only wish there had been more. You say some things that more than half persuade me you like the poems. Of course I want you to like them. I value your opinion. The only fault I find with you is that you speak with too much diffidence. You are afraid of yourself. I was impatient when you used that word "weakness" for your feeling about Pound's perfidy. You are in awe of that great intellect abloom in hair. You saw me first but you had to pass me over for him to discover. And yet compare the nice discrimination of his review of me with that of yours. Who will show me the correlation between anything I ever wrote and his quotation from the Irish, You may sit on a middan and dream stars. You may sit on a sofa and dream garters. But I must not get *libre* again. But tell me I implore what on earth is a middan if it isnt a midden and where the hell is the fitness of a word like that in connection with what I wrote on a not inexpensive farm.

One thing I'd like to ask: Did I reach you with the poems, did I get them over, as the saying is? Did I give you a feeling of and for the independent-dependence of the kind of people I like to write about. I am no propagandist of equality. But I enjoy above all things the contemplation of equality where it happily exists. I am no snob. I may be several other kinds of fool and rascal but I am not that. The John Kline who lost his housekeeper and went down like a felled ox was just the person I have described and I never knew a man I liked better—damn the world anyway.

I don't know but that I have delivered the best of what I had to say on the sound of sense. What more there may be I will be on hand to talk over with you and Hulme at five, Tuesday. My ideas got just the rub they needed last week.

Remember Mrs. Frost and me to your wife. Next time you come

out here we will have a vegetarian dish of the American Indian called succotash. Do you know it?

Sincerely yours,
R Frost.

TO F. S. FLINT

In 1909 F. S. Flint published his first volume of poems, In the Net of the Stars. *When Frost and Flint first met at Monro's Bookshop Frost bought a copy of the book and followed up the meeting with this letter reviewing the poems. This was the beginning of their friendship. Flint later reviewed* A Boy's Will.

The Bungalow
Beaconsfield
Bucks
Jan 21   1913

Dear Mr. Flint:—

I trust there was nothing ambiguous in my rather frank enjoyment of an unusual situation the other night. Considering certain gentle gibes you dealt me, I am not quite sure in the retrospect that you didn't think I was laughing at someone or something, as the American newspapers laughed (some of them) at Yeats. You will take my word for it that there was nothing in my sleeve: I showed just what I felt. I was only too childishly happy in being allowed to make one for a moment in a company in which I hadn't to be ashamed of having written verse. Perhaps it will help you understand my state of mind if I tell you that I have lived for the most part in villages where it were better that a millstone were hanged about your neck than that you should own yourself a minor poet.

About your book. Promise not to suspect me of reviewing it, as of obligation, because I bought it so ostentatiously under your eyes, and I will tell you in a word what I think of it. Poet-like you are going to resent my praising what I want to praise in it, when it comes to details. But you won't mind my saying in general that the best of it is where it came from. And the next best is the beautiful sad figure of the title, which recurring in the body of the book and, if I recollect aright, in the poem in The English Review, gives to the whole significance. We are in the net of the stars to our sorrow as inexorably as the Olympian pair were in another net to their shame. I don't know what theory you may be committed or dedicated to as an affiliated poet of Devonshire St., but for my part give me an out-and-out metaphor. If that is old-fashioned, make the most of it. And give me a generous sprinkling of words like "brindled" for the bees, "gauze" for the sea-haze, "little mouths" for the half-opened lilac flowers, "wafer" for the moon, "silver streak" for the swan's mirrored neck and "tarnished copper" for her beak. (And by the way wasn't streak with beak a fruitful rhyme?) I am disposed to think that the image finds its word and phrase with you more nearly than it finds its cadence. That is not to say that I am not taken with the sound of what you write.

"The winds that leave to-night in peace."

There it is the cadence that does it. So also is it the cadence in the first fourteen lines of "Simplicity," and in a different way in the five-word line

"No more? But no less."

Something akin to that effect is what I go reading book after book of new poetry for—if you understand what I mean.

In closing I will name you my selection for the anthologies. Mrs Frost says "Once in Autumn"; I say "Evening" or your "Foreword." Now you have something to go on if you are determined "to have me in the number of the enemy"—the expression is that of an earlier invader of your country, in fact the earliest whose name has come down to us.

All this is uncalled-for I know. The more reason, from my point of view, for saying it. I had your book, I had your card, I had the impression of your prevailing mood, I was impelled to write, and I have written. You make me long to ask you a question that your book only makes a lovely pretense of answering. When the life of the streets perplexed me a long time ago I attempted to find an answer to it for myself by going literally into the wilderness, where I was so lost to friends and everyone that not five people crossed my threshold in as many years. I came back to do my days work in its day none the wiser.

Sincerely yours,

Robert Frost

TO F. S. FLINT

This parody-attack on Ezra Pound was one of several that Frost wrote as a safety valve for his personal irritation with him. Cautiously, he sent them to Flint rather than to Pound himself. The "twins" referred to in this unpublished poem are the husband-and-wife poets H.D. and Richard Aldington who had just been "discovered" by Pound, "the affluent American Buyer." Frost's irritation continued in the postscript that he added the following day.

The Bungalow
Beaconsfield
Bucks.
[June 23   1913]

Dear Flint:

I had a funny feeling in the region of my dorsal fin this afternoon and when I came to again I had written this debased Whit-

manese. I am impelled to show it to you. You may show it to
Pound if you think it won't get me into any worse trouble than
I deserve to get into. You could type it and show it to him for
his opinion. Say a young fellow of whom you are beginning to
have some hopes did it. Say the accents are made to go that way
on purpose just as soldiers are made to break step in crossing a
bridge for fear too much rythym will shake the bridge down.
I have another poem I could write on the subject of "knowing
my father" but I spare you.

Sincerely yours
Robert Frost

[over]

Poets are Born Not Made

My nose is out of joint
For my father-in-letters—
My father mind you—
Has been brought to bed of another poet,
And I not nine months old.
It is twins this time
And they came into the world prodigiously united in wedlock
(Dont try to visualise this.)
Already they have written their *first* poem in vers libre
And sold it within twenty-four hours.
My father-in-letters was the affluent American buyer—
There was no one to bid against him.
The merit of the poem is the new convention
That definitely locates an emotion in the belly,
Instead of scientifically in the viscera at large,
Or mid-Victorianly in the heart.
It voices a desire to grin
With the grin of a beast more scared than frightened.
For why?
Because it is a cinch that twins so well born will be able
    to sell almost anything they write.

R F.

Tuesday

Thanks for all the information of your letter of this morning. We have to consider such things. Very thoughtful of you and your wife.

We enjoyed having you here so much that I hate to have you say you can't come again. We could manage better another time. We should have sent you off earlier and on a train that starts from nearby and hasn't the same chance to be late. We hope Ianthe came up smiling for the next day.

Worse and more of it. He had a finger in the writing of his own review, did he? Damn his eyes! An arrivist from the word go. He has something to show us there. But I'm blessed if I came all the way to London to be coached in art by the likes of him. He can't teach me anything I really care to know.

But I shouldn't take his unmasking too much to heart. The thing to do is to write something. Be a poet—be a scholar. You don't need his sanction. And whatever you do don't judge him too hardly on my authority. See his new protegé's poems before you condemn them. I am not quite a fool in the matter of poetry, but I may make preposterous mistakes, as Ezra Pound manifestly made a mistake when he thought he knew how to praise my poetry for the right thing. What he saw in them isnt there and what is there he couldn't have seen or he wouldn't have liked them. I have to thank you for the word "subtlety" in your review. The poems are open. I am not so sure that the best of them are simple. If they are they are subtle too. I thank you, too, for seeing the humour. Pound would never in his life see the humour of "In a Vale." But who cares? And if I am not so very impatient of success why should you be who have the advantage of me by ten years in the race?

R F.

TO SIDNEY COX

The definiteness and astuteness of Frost's critical judgments are clearly evident here. Frost's admiration for Yeats was strong; as a teacher at Pinkerton Academy he had directed Cathleen Ni Hoolihan.

[*c.* 15 September 1913] Beaconsfield

Dear Cox:

Suppose I put off scolding you the rest till another time and allow myself the freedom in pencil of saying anything that comes into my head. I wonder if there is anything in particular you would like to know about how life goes over here and I wonder if I am mind-reader enough to guess what it would be.

There is Yates you spoke of as being rated by the departmental professor considerably below that good boy from Oxford, the sing-songing (as distinguished from the song-singing) Alfie No-yes. Do you want to hear what I think of him? If you are where you can lay hands on the Oxford Book of Victorian Verse I can talk to you from that. It gives Noyes plenty of space to show his paces. "When spring comes back to England" is pleasant enough lilt—the children like it—very likely it is the best thing Noyes has done. But no one would say that it was stirring. The second poem with the tiresome "mon bel ami" refrain expects you to be moved at the thought that Venus has settled down to suckle John Bull's baby by an English hearth. The thought is not stirring: the note is not deep enough to be stirring. Swinging is not stirring, you know. Neither is swelling necessarily stirring. The poem in which he gets Francis Thompson "purpureally enwound" swells, but who cares a pin. I wish I knew what you thought he had written that got below the surface of things. I believe he has preached a little—is preaching now on the subject of peace. I recall a poem beginning, Beyond beyond and yet again beyond! What went ye forth to seek oh foolish fond." That strikes a note. ("Foolish fond" is rather awful.) I doubt if there is very much to him however. He is nothing for the American people to rage over. His attractive manners and his press agents have given you an exaggerated idea of his importance.

Yates' lines

> "For the good are always the merry
> Save by an evil chance"

are worth all of Noyes put together.

"Who dreamed that beauty passes like a dream?" That line fairly weeps defiance to the un-ideal, if you will understand what I mean by that. The Rose of the World, The Fiddler of Dooney, The Lake Isle of Innisfree, Down by the Sally Gardens, The Song of the Wandering Aengus, the Song of the Sad Shepherd—those are all poems. One is sure of them. They make the sense of beauty ache.

> "Then nowise worship dusty deeds."

Such an untameable spirit of poetry speaks there. You must really read Yates. He is not always good. Not many of his longer things are more than interesting. But the Land of Heart[']s Desire is lovely and so is On Shadowy Waters in poetry and Cathleen Ni Hoolihan in prose.

Some one the other day was deriving all the Masefield and Gibson sort of thing from one line of Yates' Land of Heart[']s Desire"

> "The butter's at your elbow, Father Hart."

Oh Yates has undoubtedly been the man of the last twenty years in English poetry. I won't say that he is quite great judged either by the way he takes himself as an artist or by the work he has done. I am afraid he has come just short of being. The thing you mention has been against him. I shouldn't care so much—I shouldn't care at all, if it hadn't touched and tainted his poetry. Let him be as affected as he pleases if he will only write well. But you can't be affected and write entirely well. [. . .]

Sincerely yours   Robert Frost.

TO F. S. FLINT

The friendship between Frost and Flint had become strained before Frost left England, though Frost had been still concerned enough to write a short but moving note to him just prior to sailing home. He refers to that note in this letter. It never reached Flint. It is now in the Dartmouth College Library, and is published in Lawrance Thompson's Selected Letters of Robert Frost (Letter 101). In this letter, a year and a half later, Frost is trying to re-establish the relationship. The poets referred to are the Imagists (H.D., Richard Aldington, D. H. Lawrence, Amy Lowell, and John Gould Fletcher), to whose cause Flint felt allied. The English poets Wilfred Gibson and Lascelles Abercrombie were neighbors of the Frosts in Gloucestershire. Edgar Lee Masters had published Spoon River Anthology *in 1915.*

Franconia N.H.

August 24　1916

Dear Flint:

You and a bare one or two others are England to me. It will be you I shall be going back to when I go back to England. It won't be Gibson and Monro. You didn't think it would, now did you?

I've had your two Anthologies out a good many times lately with visitors, particularly for your poems in them and more particularly for your Trees, Gloom and Easter. I wrung Gloom from you by betraying Pound. I'm a very little ashamed of myself now. But make allowances for me.

Some of your allies I have always seen: Aldington and H.D. and Lawrence. Amy Lowell will do. At any rate, she's useful to your party as trans-Atlantic Barker and politician in the ring. She sometimes gets something. I suppose some of you like her Whoop-la! But on what principle, I wonder, did you let in Fletcher. It must have been a principle of rhetoric or oratory. There are some people you have to lay it down to that poetry is in things—things that

happen to you and things that occur to you without your seeking.
I should never want to say anything else to the like of Fletcher.
I know there are others you have to turn right around the other
way with and tell them that poetry lies in words or the way things
affect you. You sit on a bent pin, for example, and what is of
importance to literature is not the pin itself but the words struck
out of you by the pin. But oh dear. I only mean that Fletcher is
a rotter willing to profess what he cant understand and to cant in
terms of Imagism for the sake of being allowed.

I suppose I oughtn't to have expected you to send your little book
of translations till I told you where I was. Come on with it. Lesley
and I are fairly deep in our Latin. You know my weakness for
Virgil's Eclogues. I believe I like the Georgics a good deal too.
But you are all for intenser poets than Virgil.

Poor dear Gibson! Whatever else has been corrupting me since
last I saw you bare headed in Oxford St. it hasn't been Gibson.
No sooner had I got down into the country near him than I began
defining my position with regard to him—and you know what that
means. It means sheering off from him. Abercrombie was another
sort. I really liked him, though I saw less of him than I saw of his
house. He lent us his house to live in that last winter when he went
off to live with the Hewletts.

After all it's all in guts—or nearly all. Of course I would have
the guts kept in. You won't misunderstand me.

Not Masters. He went about it wrong. How would he hope to
succeed in a string of things done all in one mood and on one
formula. Childish formula too: All apparently good people are bad,
and all apparently bad are good. That and Watch your wife.
Perhaps some novelty lies in asserting that she will bear watching
as much as in the days of the horns joke. But pay no attention to
me. You know how hard to please I must be at forty odd.

You wont mind if I give Edward Thomas your address? I want
him to look you up and describe you to me sometime. He's more
or less a wanderer since he enlisted or I could give you his address.
I believe he's just gone into the artillery. I wish you two fellows
could like each other a little on account of me, who am your
common loss.

I keep somewhere about me a very melancholy letter I wrote

you the night we lay in the Mersy River at Liverpool to send ashore before we sailed. No mail was permitted to go ashore, so you never got the letter. Some time when we meet again, here or there, we will open it together to see just how melancholy I was that night when I thought of myself of leaving you behind me. It is sealed in an envelope of the American Liner St Paul.

Here or there, I say. I wish I could get you where I could show you our farm in the mountains. Our forty five acres of land runs up the mountain behind the house about half a mile. In front of us the ground falls away two or three hundred feet to the very flat flood plain of the Ammonoosuc River. Beyond that, right over against us not three miles away are Lafayette and the Franconia Range of Mountains rising to five thousand feet. Not Switzerland, but rugged enough. We are too cold to do much farming. Grass and forest trees are our products. In the hunting season we can shoot bear and deer, or buy meat of both out of the butcher's cart. One of our forest trees, the rock maple, yields the maple sugar you may have read of—worth about twice as much as white cane sugar—no longer used on the farms for general purposes, but sold mainly as a sweet in the candy stores.

You *must* come over and see it all. Others come lecturing. Why can't you?

Love to you all. I should like to see Ianthe. Is she too big a girl to ride where she did the day we were on Hamstead Heath together?

Have I let myself be too nasty to some of my contemporaries. War is war and sometimes I think peace is too. Damn, there goes an epigramn.

You may and you may not find a piece of MS in this—all will depend on how I happen to feel when I am sealing up. If you do, it will be something about conscientious voting done for the divil of it in an insuffragable mood. Got to vote pretty soon for Wilson or the same man with a different name.

Yours more than ever

Robert Frost

Franconia N.H.   U.S.A.   finds me.

TO EDWIN ARLINGTON ROBINSON

Edwin Arlington Robinson's play The Porcupine *was published in 1915 Frost's appraisal of it here is in line with his own ideas on the importance of the speaking voice. Robinson remained the only contemporary poet to whom Frost gave unqualified approval.*

13 June 1915 Franconia

Dear Robinson:

Don't think I have been all this time trying to decide what your play is if it isnt a comedy. I have read it twice over but in no perplexity. It is good writing, or better than that, good speaking caught alive—every sentence of it. The speaking tones are all there on the printed page, nothing is left for the actor but to recognize and give them. And the action is in the speech where it should be, and not along beside it in antics for the body to perform. I wonder if you agree with me that the best sentences are those that convey their own tone—that haven't to be described in italics. "With feline demureness" for instance is well imagined as it is, but do you suppose it wouldnt have been possible to make the sentence to follow indicate in itself the vocal posture you had in mind. I don't say. I see a danger, of course, not unlike the danger of trying to make the dialogue describe the dress and personal appearance and give the past history of the characters. This in no spirit of fault-finding. I merely propose a question that interests me a good deal of late.

I have had to tell a number of people in my day what I thought of their writing. You are one of the few I have wanted to tell— one of the very few. Now I have my chance to tell you. I have had some sort of real satisfaction in everything of yours I have read. I hope I make that sweeping enough.

I owe Braithwaite a great deal for our meeting that day.

Always yours   Robert Frost

TO AMY LOWELL

This letter captures much of the ambivalence in Frost's relationship with Amy Lowell (1874–1925). The defensive applause is directed at Miss Lowell's book of poems Sword Blades and Poppy Seed, *published in 1914.*

13 August 1915 Franconia

My dear Miss Lowell:

There is an ominous note in your letter that seems to tell me you are getting ready to throw me over as a poet of the elect ostensibly on the ground that I am become a Best-seller when really it will be because I haven't convinced you that I like your book. What's the use of my trying to say anything now when I am in a corner? You will be sure to ascribe my prettiest compliments to fear. But I leave it to [Joseph Warren] Beach if I didn't tell him I liked the book when I was a free agent. You know my little weakness for dramatic tones. I go so far as to say that there is no poetry of any kind that is not made of dramatic tones. Your poetry always speaks. I wish sometimes you would leave to Browning some of the broader intonations he preempted. The accent-on-the-you sort of thing. But that's a small matter (or not so large as it might be): the great thing is that you and some of the rest of us have landed with both feet on all the little chipping poetry of awhile ago. We have busted 'em up as with cavalry. We have, we have we have. Yes I like your book and all I lay up against you is that you will not allow me a sense of humor. Occurs to me a simple way to make you: I could make up my mind to stand outside your Poetry Society until you did.

Sincerely yours,   Robert Frost

TO LOUIS UNTERMEYER

In 1916 Louis Untermeyer sent to Frost, for his opinion, several poems by Clement Wood which were being considered for publication in The Seven Arts. *Frost and Untermeyer were both on the advisory board of this ambitious but short-lived journal. Wood (1888–1950) was a talented young southerner who had come to New York and dabbled—among other things—in poetry. Note Frost's attack on clichés in this letter, his insistence that words have to be continually renewed to have any meaning at all. An unpublished lecture that Frost delivered at the Browne and Nichols School on March 13, 1918 was entitled "The Unmade Word: Fetching and Far-fetching." He uses the same word "fetched" here to describe that imaginative, personal, discovery of words that is essential to good poetry.*

Franconia N.H.
October 13   1916

Dear Louis:

   I can't make any of these seem very important. "Prelude" may be one or two things. I'm sure the rest are nothing distinct. The adjectives taken anywhere give the case away. It cost no effort of any kind to bring "vagrant" to "hair" nor "garish" to "day" nor "sultry" to "summer." They were all there already. Somebody fetched them sometime from a good way, no doubt, at considerable expense of spirit; but it wasn't Clement Wood. It's the same all the way through: Clement gets out of it too easily. He simply ought to be made to learn (without being told) that he must narrow down to what he actually catches himself at, to what he finds *himself* forced to think, feel, say, and do in mid-career. It will reduce his output for a while. It will make him feel pretty fragmentary—as if he hadn't enough to round out a whole of anything. Then let him be as fragmentary as he feels.

   The last two lines of "Prelude" are bad. I should wish to get rid of "As I lie aching for the touch of you," as well.

   Sorry to have to say it of Clement.

R.F.

TO RÉGIS MICHAUD

This letter was written in the flyleaf of a copy of North of Boston
*which Frost presented to Régis Michaud (1880–1939), Associate Pro-
fessor of French at Smith College and, later, author of two books on
Emerson. It suggests something of Frost's debt to Emerson.*

[*c*. January 1918] [Amherst]

Some twenty-two lines in "Monadnoc" beginning "Now in
sordid weeds they sleep" (I dont need to copy them out for such
an Emersonian as you, Michaud) meant almost more to me than
anything else on the art of writing when I was a youngster; and
that not just on the art of writing colloquial verse but on the art
of writing any kind of verse or prose. I suffer from the way people
abuse the word colloquial. All writing, I dont care how exalted,
how lyrical, or how seemingly far removed from the dramatic,
must be as colloquial as this passage from "Monadnoc" comes to.
I am as sure that the colloquial is the root of every good poem
as I am that the national is the root of all thought and art. It may
shoot up as high as you please and flourish as widely abroad in the
air, if only the roots are what and where they should be. One
half of individuality is locality: and I was about venturing to say
the other half was colloquiality. The beauty of the high thinking
in Emerson's Uriel and Give All to Love is that it is well within
the colloquial as I use the word. And so also is all the lyric in
Palgrave's Treasury for that matter, no matter at what level of
sentiment it is pitched. Consider Herrick's To Daffodils. But sometime more of this when we can sit down together.

Robert Frost

TO JOHN ERSKINE

John Erskine (1879–1951) was a teacher, editor, musician, and novelist. Though he won great popularity as a writer of iconoclastic novels set in classical times (e.g., The Private Life of Helen of Troy, published in 1925), he once confided to Frost that he would rather make a reputation as a poet than anything else, and over the years he seems to have sent Frost many poems for his critical advice. The references in this undated letter are vague: Charlie Cobb was a mutual friend at Amherst; the quoted line is perhaps from a poem Frost destroyed or perhaps was simply composed as an example while Frost was writing the letter. The "title poem" is probably "New Hampshire."

[Ann Arbor ?]
[1923 ?]

Dear Erskine:

I'm often crossed with just such doubts myself. Why will I perform such tricks on the honest old blank verse with my eyes open? It must be because I'm tempted beyond my strength. It is my way of wickedly sinning. The more I resolve not to do it the more inevitably I seem to do it when my blood is up. I suppose I'm a self-shocker. I used to get all the excitement I craved out of making lines like this:

      ᴗ ᴗ   _   _ ᴗ _ ᴗ ᴗ ᴗ   _
On the white wall presented to the road.

I think you can probably find lines as extravagant as that in almost anybody's blank verse. It's but the next step beyond _ᴗᴗ_ᴗ_ ᴗᴗᴗ_ which is to be found ever[y]where and which is responsible for Charlie Cobb's theory of tettrameters. The hanker of my sophisticated ear is always luring me further. I admit that

                         ´   ´   ´   ´   ´
            On the side it presented to the road

is out of bounds.

We won't insist too much on the title poem. You and I know enough to know a lark when we see one with a legband. It all comes down to a few lyrics, when all's said,—and a few such things in blank verse as Birches, The Mountain, The Census-taker, An Old Mans Winter Night, and probably, in spite of its faults to the ear, The Death of the Hired Man.

So very much about me for once to show you that what you think of me isnt much worse than what I think of myself.

I'm grateful for what you wrote

Ever yours
Robert Frost

TO JOHN ERSKINE

Frost's comments on Erskine's unpublished poem "Metaneira" reflect his constant interest in "the play of blank verse," and—more specifically—his concern for giving poetic themes a local habitation and a name.

South Shaftsbury Vt
July 7   1921

My dear Erskine:

You are not to think I have forgotten my engagements of the night you so sympathetically waked my poor dead Phi Beta Kappa poem with me. I was to tell you when I felt like it what I made of your Metaneira. All I can say is I hope I may have a chance in the way of business to tell a publisher sometime what I make of such another. You knew the play of blank verse wouldn't be thrown away on me. I have an idea it was the blank verse you were principally interested in hearing what I would say to. Of course it's lovely. You never fail to get something out of the relation of sentence to line. And the theme is lovely too, of the too maternal mother who from want of faith in the natural misses for her child the gift of the spiritual.

But why to objectify the idea and put it far enough away from yourself must you put it away off in antiquity and say it in heroes and gods. Why must you every time, I mean. All right for this poem; but why not next time say it in modern people. It is like diffidence, shyness, this remoteness in time and space. Get over it and you can break in on the age with your strength and insight. I'll bet I'm right.

Sincerely yours
Robert Frost

TO LOUIS UNTERMEYER

The running commentary that Frost gives in this letter is directed at the contributing poets, including the editor himself, to Untermeyer's first Miscellany of American Poetry, published in 1920. "The Pollywog" is Frost's jocular title for Untermeyer's "Boy and Tadpoles." "The Long Hill" and "Water Lilies" were written by Sara Teasdale. Amy Lowell contributed a nine-page poem "Funeral Song for the Indian Chief Blackbird." Edwin Arlington Robinson's poem was an eight-line lyric "The Dark Hills," which Frost later q oted in his own tribute to Robinson, the King Jasper preface. James Oppenheim's contribution, "The Man Who Would Be God," dealt with Woodrow Wilson. "Jean" is Untermeyer's wife Jean Starr. The comments on Vachel Lindsay, Carl Sandburg, and John Gould Fletcher are self-explanatory. "Shinleaf" was a poem that Untermeyer dedicated to Frost.

Franconia N.H.
July 17   1920

Dear Louis:

If you have enough poems like The New Adam and A Marriage to make up a volume without the help of anything else of any other kind, you can set yourself so far apart from anyone else that you won't even need boundary lines let alone stone walls to mark you off. I don't know where else to look for that full-savoring sensuousness of thirty years that ploughs where twenty used to tickle. It would be one thing to do and of course you would do it well. Why plan to have a little of everything (as I'll bet you do) in your next book. Why not hew to the idea of your title, however small a book it leaves you for a dollar and a half? Don't have The Pollywog in it for instance. Save the Pollywog to go with The Frog when you shall write it.

Intercession is the lovely one of the lot. But I don't know that you want to be encouraged to be lovely in that sense. Being lovely might interfere with being energetic, which is what you always give the effect of being at your best even in such a thing as the Pollywog. And no matter whom you translate he comes through you energized and more energetic than he went in. It would be foolish not to reckon with that and not make yourself out of what you are.

While I am about it I may as well have my shot at the other contributors to your Misc. When shall I listen to anything I like better than The Long Hill and the Water Lilies. The perfect accent. And neither of them the least bit wrested to bring in Sappho or the bursting heart. You must forgive me for liking these two poems about as well as anything you have in the book.

Vachel I don't have to deal with because these poems have been withdrawn. I tried to read his Golden Whales aloud in company last night. It failed to get me by the hyperbolics.

All I want to say about Amy is she had better enquire of the Smithsonian Institute if the Indian or any other American but H.D. (and she's an expatriate) wails in the two separate vowels "a" and "i" after the Greeks. Her poem on the resolute young men you can't have too much of in this world reminds me of one on A Pair of Pants a lady of Europe wrote before the war made atrocities popular. She was said to dance it out as Duncan was then dancing verse. It went:

> We women are restricted to a glance
> At where the virile member bags the pants.

I only remember the authoress wasn't Felicia Hemans. Anyway Amy is more exciting when she calls for young men not incapable than when she takes five hundred thin lines to bury an Indian Chief on horseback. No to her. The Chief is buried all right.

Carl's idiom and lingo would be enough if there was nothing else in the book. He's a box of pen points. Gimme Aprons of Silence; Crapshooters; Man, the Man Hunter; Blue Island Intersection; and Pencils.

Robinson the cunning devil isn't forgetting his effects when he pretends to have only the one small poem to be lost among our many. I'd like to punish him for his selfish calculation if I could see where to strike. But I don't unless it is his calling the sunset a sound for the rhyme.

Fletcher is a whole lot better than I expected him to be. I have mixed him up too much with Amy to be fair to him.

There's a lot of good in Aiken. Maybe it's all good (though never the thriller that the Morning Song of Senlin is); but it is too formidable, especially for leading off with. Our misfortune more than his that his name begins with an A. You couldn't get him further into the book by arranging us in some other order on some other principle? Beans is a good Boston subject, and the beans are the best part of the poem. Wouldn't I be likely to say so?

James should have read again what Korah said to Moses and then written his denunciation of Woodrow. "You take too much upon you seeing all the congregation (namely the Senate) are holy everyone of them and the Lord is among them: wherefore then lift you up yourself above the congregation of the Lord?" "Is it a small thing that thou hast brought us up out of a land that floweth with milk and honey to kill us in the wilderness except thou make thyself altogether a prince over us?" You remember what happened to Korah and his friends and his wives and his sons and his little children. I was brought up on that.

There remains only Jean to speak of. Why will she let the spirit be dragged down sick by the sick body? If the spirit were sick in its own right I shouldn't be preaching this sermon. But it is the body uttering its sickness through the spirit—I can tell by the sound. I suppose I should distrust any sickness of the spirit as from the body unless I knew for certain that the body had a clean bill of health from the medical dept. A sick spirit in a sound body for me. It's a personal preference I am expressing. No doubt a sick spirit in a sick body has its honor and its reward. So much for the subject matter apart from the poeticality of the poetry. Of course I know the poems are truthful close and workmanlike.

If it were My Misc I'm pretty sure I would jumble the poetry in it. I'd begin with a real lady, say Jean or Sara; go over us once in one order and then in another. It would look less like the Georgian and it would get rid of Aiken's solid thing lying across the threshold.

Thanks from the heart for "Shinleaf." Some day when you have given me up as cold and ungrateful I shall requite it.

Ever yours
Robert Frost

[Postscript omitted]

TO WITTER BYNNER

Witter Bynner (1881–1968) was an American poet and translator whom Frost met in 1921. His books include The Grenstone Poems *(1919),* A Book of Love *(a translation from the French of Charles Vildrac—1923);* Indian Earth *(1929), and* The Jade Mountain *(a translation of Chinese poetry—1929). In 1916, under the pseudonym Emanuel Morgan, he contributed to a satirical collection of parodies of modern poetry called* Spectra—*a hoax which was for a time considered a serious contribution to contemporary verse experiments.*

Frost's comments here on the nature of translations are valuable in the light of his statement that poetry is "that which is lost out of both prose and verse in translation." They assert his basic belief in the integrity of poetic form.

South Shaftsbury Vermont
June 29   1930

Dear Witter:

I'd so much rather talk to you than write to you that I suffer in the comparison. But that is no excuse for my not having written long ago to thank you for the books you sent and tell you that I remain your faithful admirer in almost everything you do.

It fascinates me to watch the way your different selves influence each other. You are a self-suggestible. Taking your Grenstone self as the norm, we all know what your Spectral self did to that. And now we have displayed in the Chapala poems what the translator-from-the-Chinese in you has done to it. I confess translations from the Chinese or any other language bother me with questions. (Your translation from the French of Vildrac was one of the few I ever forgot myself in.) I can't help wondering all the time I read if the vapidity of translation from the Chinese, for instance, is a fault or virtue of the original, the childlike blandness that Truthful James celebrates in the Oriental, or merely a fault acquired in dispensing with the form of the original. I cant help suspecting that something goes when the form the poem is conceived in goes. I have thought and thought and thought about it. I like your Chinese poems well, better than other people's. But I like better still your own free-hand performance in the spirit of the Chinese. (It probably enhances the Chapala Poems that D. H. Lawrence has died since I read them first, that the very first poem I ever wrote myself (1890) was about how the children of Quetzal and Huitzil once gave Cortés One Very Bad Night, and that some of my earliest reading and some of my latest was-is John L. Stephens Yucatan.) In other words with a little help from the Chinese you have made an exotic more to my taste out of Old Mexico than with a great deal of help from the Chinese you have made out of old China. You must indulge my prejudice— my body it is fifty-six. Chinese poetry when I came across it gave me a scare for my notion of all poetry, that it was nothing but metaphor, the heaven-appointed way of saying one thing and meaning another, instead of meaning what you said. But Chinese poetry comes in under the definition all right, only perhaps too unvaryingly with the figure Suggestion. I've been impressed by Chinese poetry. Of course something gets across to us from it. I can imagine anything of it in the original. But I'll bet a poetry-prize I am nearer that magic in your Chapala poems than in your translations, just as I am nearer Grecian magic in Arnolds Cadmus and Harmonia, written under the influence of the Greek, than I am in anything Gilbert Murray George Palmer Butcher Lang or anybody else ever translated from the Greek. I shall be reading your Chinese translations again sometime and will report any change of mind.

Thus are we torn in conflict between agate and jade—taking sides now with agate. It is forbidden us as neither Yaqui nor Mongol but Christian, to wish by dying to be made careless of agate careless of jade. Too soon we'll be careless of everything, even of each other may be, though I refuse to give in entirely to the fear. At least let it not be while we live.

Faithfully
Robert Frost

TO LEONIDAS W. PAYNE JR.

Leonidas W. Payne Jr. (1873–1945) was Chairman of the English Department at the University of Texas, and entertained the Frosts on their visit to Texas in 1922. When Frost's Collected Poems was published in 1930, Payne sent Frost a list of "errors" which he found in the volume. Frost's reply reveals his barely-restrained annoyance at such misguided, if well-meant, intervention, and asserts his conscious discarding of "school-girl English."

[c. November 1930] [South Shaftsbury]

Dear Payne:

I'm sorry about all those commas and hyphens. But you know I indulge a sort of indifference to punctuation. I dont mean I despise it. I value it. But I seem rather willing to let other people look after it for me. One of my prides is that I can write a fifty word telegram without having to use a single "Stop" for the sense. I'll have those commas and hyphens tended to though, if only for your peace of mind.

I must say you scared me with your formidable-looking list. Fortunately it turned out you were wrong in all your findings of errors except the punctuational. It would have been terrible if I had been off verbally grammatically or metrically. I have to be a pretty exact person when it comes to such a delicate poem as Moon Compasses. Your suggestion there would spoil my meaning. *Was measured* doesnt mean the same thing as *measured*. My passive is perfectly idiomatic. You must remember I am not writing school-girl English.

Codlin should be in your dictionary. It is a form still in use among apple men. Codling is getting the better of it as language goes more and more to school. Codlin is to codling as leggin is to legging, as interval is to intervale. *Codlin'* would look funny in any book of mine. I havent dropped a g that way in a lifetime of writing.

Substituting *but that* for *but* in "Waspish" would show school girl timidity and spoil my metrics. *But* alone will be found all the way down our literature. I noticed it tonight in Robinson Crusoe.

> Leaves and bark, leaves and bark
> To lean against and hear in the dark

The reversing of the order should remind you of a very ancient figure of speech. Your friends of the Classical Department will tell you about it. I dont want to seem pedantic.

Inserting *its* after *doubt* on page 87 would be school girl English to my ear. I give you credit for being able to supply words plainly understood. Dialogue would be unendurable if all words had to be said outright for complete construction.

No not a word has been dropped out or printed wrong I believe. There was one terrible mistake in the first edition of West-running Brook: roams for romps. One of my friends liked the printers accident better than my intention. Anyway he resented the correction when it was made in the Collected. He was duly embarrassed when he learned how it was. He neednt have been. I didnt mind the criticism implied.

Well here's thinking of you gratefully for all your trouble with

proof-reading the book and for reviewing it so finely. I wonder
what form of it you lack and would like me to send you. You
know Im   Always yours faithfully   Robert Frost

TO CAROL FROST

*Carol was Frost's only son to survive childhood. Although some of
his poems are extant, and are held by Mrs. Lesley Frost Ballantine,
"Stratton" seems to have been lost.*

[*c.* 18 March 1933] [Amherst]

Dear Carol:

Your Stratton poem is powerful and splendid. You have ham-
mered it close and hard and you have rammed it full of all sorts
of things, observations both of nature and human nature—and
humor and picturesqueness too. And best of all, as Marge says,
it is no sissy poem such as I get from poetic boys generally. It is
written with a man's vigor and goes down in to a man's depth.
You perhaps don't realize what that means to me. And one thing
more: the poem is richly attractive, not repulsive and ugly the way
so many think they have to describe life now-a-days to be honest.
You are not always quite clear to me but I can put up with some
obscurity where there is so much solid truth, such condensation
and intense feeling. The clearness must be thought of. But you
mustn't sacrifice anything you now have to get clearness. Practice
in aiming at the mind of your reader will make you clearer every
day. I don't quite know for instance what touch here and there is
needed in that remarkably interesting passage about the officers in
Stratton. But it is a little too hard just as it is—a little too puzzling.
Even I who know more about the subject of more offices than
men to fill them have some trouble in working it out. In straight-
ening it out, there would be danger of losing some of the charming

twists and turns and kinks. I shouldn't want to lose those of course. How I like the smooth clarity and high sentiment of

> "The place for me"
>   "And me"

and from there on a way. I think the best of all may be the passage

> "replenished clear
> And cold from mountain streams that ever hear
> Proceeding waters calling from below."

Well you are getting a firmer grip on the art now in every way from rhyming up to packing in the ideas. (I ought to mention the way you vary the length and shape of the sentences in the lines and overlapping the lines to save yourself from monotony also.) It is a question how you can arrange your life to give yourself further opportunities to develop your poetry. You're sure are you, that you want to come east this summer? You've got a lot out of your enforced freedom from heavy farming. Perhaps you've got out all you can for the present. Its worth giving a lot of thought to before you act.

We were impatient to hear about you folks in the earthquake [Long Beach, 10 March 1933]. Prescott's letter came first. Now that you have had an earthquake in California you may feel shaken down into a firmer affection for the state. Marge heard someone say that the whole state was just a shelf over the ocean that would some day fall in and sink. And the expression "on the shelf" for a retired person came from there being so many retired people in California.

Affectionately,   Papa

TO LOUIS UNTERMEYER

James Agee (1909–1955) published his first volume of poems Permit
Me Voyage *in the Yale Series of Younger Poets in 1934. Untermeyer
sent Frost a copy, and this is Frost's reply. The long psychological
poem referred to in the beginning of his letter is "Ann Garner," and
the "first little lyric" is an unnamed poem that runs as follows:*

> *Child, should any pleasant boy*
> *Find you lovely, many could,*
> *Wind not up between your joy*
> *The sly delays of maidenhood:*
>
> *Spread all your beauty in his sight*
> *And do him kindness every way,*
> *Since soon, too soon, the wolfer night*
> *Climbs in between, and ends fair play.*

Amherst Mass
November 2   1934

Dear Louis:

[. . .] And now Agee—Oh gee! Ain't that long one a terrible travesty of Birches, Home Burial, and The Fear combined!
And the psychology of having a woman so bothered over a still-
born child! Take the very first little lyric in the book. What is
such a thing if it isn't pretty flawless? There are five flaws to eight
lines. You can't have anything between a joy—one joy. "Many
could" is painful outside parenthesis. The euphuism of "everyway"
is unpleasant. Why not say every which way? What does "wind
not up" mean? I've heard this being kind to a boy called winding
up a little ball of yarn. Wolfer night doesn't interrupt love. Night
brings lovers together. He means wolfer *day*. Of course he means
Death, if you'll only help him with a little understanding. "Climbs!"
Why climbs? No luck at all in my first two dips. What am I going
to say to the kid? "Hereafter in a better book than this I shall
desire more love and knowledge of you."

R.

TO AMY BONNER

The whimsy that Frost's criticism could lapse into, as well as the wit of his punning, is delightfully demonstrated in these comments on Wallace Stevens' "A Rabbit as King of the Ghosts" and Robert Penn Warren's "Bearded Oaks," both published in Poetry: A Magazine of Verse *in October, 1937.*

Bay St North
Gainesville Florida
Dec 14   1937

Dear Miss Bonner:

I wondered what had come over Poetry that it should be going in for interviews and special personal numbers. Dont let it trouble you that nothing could come of your friendly enthusiasm to promote me. We all like people who make mistakes of your kind; and you shall be rewarded with a poem for the magazine just as soon as I can give it the parting touch. Thanks for the two last Poetries under Zabel. I lent myself to them for several hours. First I was a swelling rabbit with my old class mate Wallace Stevens. I believe I never so entered into the moonlight life of a rabbit before. And the swelling of its ego. So Freudian. Next I was a submarine atoll with Robert Penn Warren. It took some thought to achieve that identification. But it was worth it. My weakness is that I like to think hard and deep. How many fathoms deep do you suppose that atoll was meant to lie? I feel as if I had been down there and much benefited. I'm afraid you'll put me down for a fraudian. My opinion is (if you ask it) that a poet like George Dillon will be the best editor Poetry has had since Harriet in her best days.

Sincerely yours
Robert Frost

TO KIMBALL FLACCUS

Kimball Flaccus (1911–   ) is a New England poet, and a graduate of Dartmouth College. His work includes In Praise of Mara *(1932),* Avalanche of April *(1934), and contributions to various New England anthologies. Over the years he sought Frost's advice about his poetry. This letter, written in Elinor Frost's handwriting, reveals the paternalistic interest that Frost showed in younger poets whom he could regard as protégés. In it he establishes clearly the sources of poetic inspiration.*

15 Sunset Ave.
Amherst
Nov. 26th [1932?]

Dear Flaccus,—

I have been sick in bed for a week—and am still unable to write letters. I am sorry to have kept your poem so long. I have had one or two good looks at it, and should like to see it again when it is finished. The best of it is the passage about the Barre stone cutter out of hospital. You realize yourself that is first rate material for poetry of this kind. There are a lot of things I could say to you about the art if we were talking, and one of them is that it should be of major adventures only, outward or inward—important things that happen to you, or important things that occur to you. Mere poeticality won't suffice. We must wait for things to happen to us big, or occur to us big. We are sure to have some big luck if we wait long enough. At almost any age we are pretty sure to find on looking back we have had more big luck than we knew. The main point is that I put the two on equal terms, the things that happen to you and the things that occur to you. You can't have them at will, but they are certainties now and then in any life of living and thinking. And when you get a good one, given out of nowhere, you can almost trust it to do itself in poetry. Almost, I say. You can at least seem to throw away all you ever learned in your long apprenticeship to formal beauty. But we can talk more when I see you. I am dictating this to you—

Always yours.

Robert Frost

TO *THE AMHERST STUDENT*

When the editors of The Amherst Student *sent greetings to Frost for his "sixtieth" (actually his sixty-first) birthday in 1935, Frost wrote this reply, which was printed in that undergraduate paper on 25 March, 1935. It is one of his most memorable statements on form as a philosophical necessity.*

[*c.* 21 March 1935] [Key West]

It is very very kind of the *Student* to be showing sympathy with me for my age. But sixty is only a pretty good age. It is not advanced enough. The great thing is to be advanced. Now ninety would be really well along and something to be given credit for.

But speaking of ages, you will often hear it said that the age of the world we live in is particularly bad. I am impatient of such talk. We have no way of knowing that this age is one of the worst in the world's history. Arnold claimed the honor for the age before this. Wordsworth claimed it for the last but one. And so on back through literature. I say they claimed the honor for their ages. They claimed it rather for themselves. It is immodest of a man to think of himself as going down before the worst forces ever mobilized by God.

All ages of the world are bad—a great deal worse anyway than Heaven. If they weren't the world might just as well be Heaven at once and have it over with. One can safely say after from six to thirty thousand years of experience that the evident design is a situation here in which it will always be about equally hard to save your soul. Whatever progress may be taken to mean, it can't mean making the world any easier a place in which to save your soul—or if you dislike hearing your soul mentioned in open meeting, say your decency, your integrity.

Ages may vary a little. One may be a little worse than another. But it is not possible to get outside the age you are in to judge it exactly. Indeed it is as dangerous to try to get outside of anything as large as an age as it would be to engorge a donkey. Witness the many who in the attempt have suffered a dilation from which the tissues and the muscles of the mind have never been able to recover natural shape. They can't pick up anything delicate or small any more. They can't use a pen. They have to use a typewriter. And they gape in agony. They can write huge shapeless novels, huge gobs of raw sincerity bellowing with pain and that's all that they can write.

Fortunately we don't need to know how bad the age is. There is something we can always be doing without reference to how good or how bad the age is. There is at least so much good in the world that it admits of form and the making of form. And not only admits of it, but calls for it. We people are thrust forward out of the suggestions of form in the rolling clouds of nature. In us nature reaches its height of form and through us exceeds itself. When in doubt there is always form for us to go on with. Anyone who has achieved the least form to be sure of it, is lost to the larger excruciations. I think it must stroke faith the right way. The artist, the poet, might be expected to be the most aware of such assurance, but it is really everybody's sanity to feel it and live by it. Fortunately, too, no forms are more engrossing, gratifying, comforting, staying, than those lesser ones we throw off like vortex rings of smoke, all our individual enterprise and needing nobody's cooperation: a basket, a letter, a garden, a room, an idea, a picture, a poem. For these we haven't to get a team together before we can play.

The background is hugeness and confusion shading away from where we stand into black and utter chaos; and against the background any small man-made figure of order and concentration. What pleasanter than that this should be so? Unless we are novelists or economists we don't worry about this confusion; we look out on it with an instrument or tackle it to reduce it. It is partly because we are afraid it might prove too much for us and our blend of democratic-republican-socialist-communist-anarchist party. But it is more because we like it, we were born to it, born used to it and have practical reasons for wanting it there. To me any little form I assert upon it is velvet, as the saying is, and to be considered for how much more it is than nothing. If I were a Platonist I should have to consider it, I suppose, for how much less it is than everything.

Prefaces

INTRODUCTION TO *THE ARTS ANTHOLOGY: DARTMOUTH VERSE, 1925*

This preface has not been reprinted since it first appeared in 1925. It surely deserves renewed recognition for the striking working-out of its central image as well as for Frost's characteristic upsetting of the contemporary educational applecart.

No one given to looking under-ground in spring can have failed to notice how a bean starts its growth from the seed. Now the manner of a poet's germination is less like that of a bean in the ground than of a waterspout at sea. He has to begin as a cloud of all the other poets he ever read. That can't be helped. And first the cloud reaches down toward the water from above and then the water reaches up toward the cloud from below and finally cloud and water join together to roll as one pillar between heaven and earth. The base of water he picks up from below is of course all the life he ever lived outside of books.

These, then, are the three figures of the waterspout, and the first is about as far as the poet doomed to die young in everyone of us usually gets. He brings something down from Dowson, Yeats, Morris, Masefield, or the Imagists (often a long way down), but lifts little or nothing up. If he were absolutely certain to do as doomed and die young, he would hardly be worth getting excited over in college or elsewhere. But you can't be too careful about whom you will ignore in this world. Cases have been known of his refusing at the last minute to abdicate the breast in favor of the practical and living on to write lyric like Landor till ninety.

Right in this book he will be found surviving into the second figure of the waterspout, and, by several poems and many scattered lines, even into the third figure. *The Heritage, Sonnet, I Have Built* a *Vessel,* and *The Wanderer,* good as they are of their kind—accomplished and all that—are of the first figure and frankly derivative. They are meant to do credit to anyone's reading. But *The Letter, The Village Daily, For a Salvationist,* and best of all, *The Ski Jumper,* at least get up the salt water. Their realism represents an advance. They show acceptance of the fact that the way to better is often through worse. In such a poem as *Underneath Sleep* the pillar revolves pretty much unbroken.

We are here getting a long way with poetry, considering all there is against it in school and college. The poet, as everyone knows, must strike his individual note sometime between the ages of fifteen and twenty-five. He may hold it a long time, or a short time, but it is then he must strike it or never. School and college have been conducted with the almost express purpose of keeping him busy with something else till the danger of his ever creating anything is past. Their motto has been, the muses find some mischief still for idle hands to do. No one is asking to see poetry regularized in courses and directed by coaches like sociology and football. It must remain a theft to retain its savor. But it does seem as if it could be a little more connived at than it is. I for one should be in favor of the colleges setting the expectation of poetry forward a few years (the way the clocks are set forward in May), so as to get the young poets started earlier in the morning before the freshness dries off. Just setting the expectation of poetry forward might be all that was needed to give us our proportioned number of poets to Congressmen.

R.F.

INTRODUCTION TO *KING JASPER*

When Edwin Arlington Robinson's poem King Jasper *was published in 1935, shortly after Robinson's death, Frost was asked to write a preface to it, as a posthumous tribute to a poet he greatly admired. It is one of Frost's most astute pieces of literary criticism.*

It may come to the notice of posterity (and then again it may not) that this, our age, ran wild in the quest of new ways to be new. The one old way to be new no longer served. Science put it into our heads that there must be new ways to be new. Those tried were largely by subtraction—elimination. Poetry, for example, was tried without punctuation. It was tried without capital letters. It was tried without metric frame on which to measure the rhythm. It was tried without any images but those to the eye; and a loud general intoning had to be kept up to cover the total loss of specific images to the ear, those dramatic tones of voice which had hitherto constituted the better half of poetry. It was tried without content under the trade name of poesie pure. It was tried without phrase, epigram, coherence, logic and consistency. It was tried without ability. I took the confession of one who had had deliberately to unlearn what he knew. He made a back-pedalling movement of his hands to illustrate the process. It was tried premature like the delicacy of unborn calf in Asia. It was tried without feeling or sentiment like murder for small pay in the underworld. These many things was it tried without, and what had we left? Still something. The limits of poetry had been sorely strained, but the hope was that the idea had been somewhat brought out.

Robinson stayed content with the old-fashioned way to be new. I remember bringing the subject up with him. How does a man come on his difference, and how does he feel about it when he first finds it out? At first it may well frighten him, as his difference with the Church frightened Martin Luther. There is such a thing as being too willing to be different. And what shall we say to people who are not only willing but anxious? What assurance have they that their difference is not insane, eccentric, abortive, unintelligible? Two fears should follow us through life. There is the fear that we shan't prove worthy in the eyes of someone who knows us at least as well as we know ourselves. That is the fear of God. And there is the fear of Man—the fear that men won't understand us and we shall be cut off from them.

We begin in infancy by establishing correspondence of eyes with eyes. We recognized that they were the same feature and we could do the same things with them. We went on to the visible motion of the lips—smile answered smile; then cautiously, by trial and error, to compare the invisible muscles of the mouth and throat. They were the same and could make the same sounds. We were still together. So far, so good. From here on the wonder grows. It has been said that recognition in art is all. Better say correspondence is all. Mind must convince mind that it can uncurl and wave the same filaments of subtlety, soul convince soul that it can give off the same shimmers of eternity. At no point would anyone but a brute fool want to break off this correspondence. It is all there is to satisfaction; and it is salutary to live in the fear of its being broken off.

The latest proposed experiment of the experimentalists is to use poetry as a vehicle of grievances against the un-Utopian state. As I say, most of their experiments have been by subtraction. This would be by addition of an ingredient that latter-day poetry has lacked. A distinction must be made between griefs and grievances. Grievances are probably more useful than griefs. I read in a sort of Sunday-school leaflet from Moscow, that the grievances of Chekhov against the sordidness and dullness of his home-town society have done away with the sordidness and dullness of home-town society all over Russia. They were celebrating the event. The grievances of the great Russians of the last century have given Russia a revolution. The grievances of their great followers in America may well give us, if not a revolution, at least some palliative pensions. We must suffer them to put life at its ugliest and forbid them not, as we value our reputation for liberality.

I had it from one of the youngest lately: "Whereas we once thought literature should be without content, we now know it should be charged full of propaganda." Wrong twice, I told him. Wrong twice and of theory prepense. But he returned to his position after a moment out for reassembly: "Surely art can be considered good only as it prompts to action." How soon, I asked him. But there is danger of undue levity in teasing the young. The experiment is evidently started. Grievances are certainly a power and are going to be turned on. We must be very tender of our dreamers. They may seem like picketers or members of the committee on rules for the moment. We shan't mind what they seem, if only they produce real poems.

But for me, I don't like grievances. I find I gently let them alone wherever published. What I like is griefs and I like them Robinsonianly profound. I suppose there is no use in asking, but I should think we might be indulged to the extent of having grievances restricted to prose if prose will accept the imposition, and leaving poetry free to go its way in tears.

Robinson was a prince of heartachers amid countless achers of another part. The sincerity he wrought in was all sad. He asserted the sacred right of poetry to lean its breast to a thorn and sing its dolefullest. Let weasels suck eggs. I know better where to look for melancholy. A few superficial irritable grievances, perhaps, as was only human, but these are forgotten in the depth of griefs to which he plunged us.

Grievances are a form of impatience. Griefs are a form of patience. We may be required by law to throw away patience as we have been required to surrender gold; since by throwing away patience and joining the impatient in one last rush on the citadel of evil, the hope is we may end the need of patience. There will be nothing left to be patient about. The day of perfection waits on unanimous social action. Two or three more good national elections should do the business. It has been similarly urged on us to give up courage, make cowardice a virtue, and see if that won't end war, and the need of courage. Desert religion for science, clean out the holes and corners of the residual unknown, and there will be no more need of religion. (Religion is merely consolation for what we don't know.) But suppose there was some mistake, and the evil stood siege, the war didn't end, and something remained unknowable. Our having disarmed would make our case worse than it had ever been before. Nothing in the latest advices from Wall Street, the League of Nations, or the Vatican incline me to give up my holdings in patient grief.

There were Robinson and I, it was years ago, and the place (near Boston Common) was the Place, as we liked afterward to call it, of Bitters, because it was with bitters, though without bitterness, we could sit there and look out on the welter of dissatisfaction and experiment in the world around us. It was too long ago to remember who said what, but the sense of the meeting was, we didn't care how arrant a reformer or experimentalist a man was if he gave us real poems. For ourselves, we should hate to be read for any theory upon which we might be supposed to write. We doubted any poem could persist for any theory upon which it might have been written. Take the theory that poetry in our language could be treated as quantitative, for example. Poems had been written in spite of it. And poems are all that matter. The utmost of ambition is to lodge a few poems where they will be hard to get rid of, to lodge a few irreducible bits where Robinson lodged more than his share.

For forty years it was phrase on phrase on phrase with Robinson, and every one the closest delineation of something that *is* something. Any poet, to resemble him in the least, would have to resemble him in that grazing closeness to the spiritual realities. If books of verse were to be indexed by lines first in importance instead of lines first in position, many of Robinson's poems would be represented several times over. This should be seen to. The only possible objection is that it could not be done by any mere hireling of the moment, but would have to be the work of someone who had taken his impressions freely before he had any notion of their use. A particular poem's being represented several times would only increase the chance of its being located.

The first poet I ever sat down with to talk about poetry was Ezra Pound. It was in London in 1913. The first poet we talked about, to the best of my recollection, was Edwin Arlington Robinson. I was fresh from America and from having read *The Town Down the River*. Beginning at that book, I have slowly spread my reading of Robinson twenty years backward and forward, about equally in both directions.

I remember the pleasure with which Pound and I laughed over the fourth "thought" in

> Miniver thought, and thought, and thought,
> And thought about it.

Three "thoughts" would have been "adequate" as the critical praise-word then was. There would have been nothing to complain of, if it had been left at three. The fourth made the intolerable touch of poetry. With the fourth, the fun began. I was taken out on the strength of our community of opinion here, to be rewarded with an introduction to Miss May Sinclair, who had quali-

fied as the patron authority on young and new poets by the
sympathy she had shown them in *The Divine Fire.*

There is more to it than the number of "thoughts." There is
the way the last one turns up by surprise round the corner, the
way the shape of the stanza is played with, the easy way the
obstacle of verse is turned to advantage. The mischief is in it.

> One pauses half afraid
> To say for certain that he played—

a man as sorrowful as Robinson. His death was sad to those who
knew him, but nowhere near as sad as the lifetime of poetry to
which he attuned our ears. Nevertheless, I say his much-admired
restraint lies wholly in his never having let grief go further than
it could in play. So far shall grief go, so far shall philosophy go,
so far shall confidences go, and no further. Taste may set the limit.
Humor is a surer dependence.

> And once a man was there all night,
> Expecting something every minute.

I know what the man wanted of Old King Cole. He wanted the
heart out of his mystery. He was the friend who stands at the end
of a poem ready in waiting to catch you by both hands with enthusiasm and drag you off your balance over the last punctuation
mark into more than you meant to say. "I understand the poem
all right, but please tell me what is behind it?" Such presumption
needs to be twinkled at and baffled. The answer must be, "If I
had wanted you to know, I should have told you in the poem."
We early have Robinson's word for it:

> The games we play
> To fill the frittered minutes of a day
> Good glasses are to read the spirit through.

He speaks somewhere of Crabbe's stubborn skill. His own was
a happy skill. His theme was unhappiness itself, but his skill was
as happy as it was playful. There is that comforting thought for

those who suffered to see him suffer. Let it be said at the risk of offending the humorless in poetry's train (for there are a few such): his art was more than playful; it was humorous.

The style is the man. Rather say the style is the way the man takes himself; and to be at all charming or even bearable, the way is almost rigidly prescribed. If it is with outer seriousness, it must be with inner humor. If it is with outer humor, it must be with inner seriousness. Neither one alone without the other under it will do. Robinson was thinking as much in his sonnet on Tom Hood. One ordeal of Mark Twain was the constant fear that his occluded seriousness would be overlooked. That betrayed him into his two or three books of out-and-out seriousness.

Miniver Cheevy was long ago. The glint I mean has kept coming to the surface of the fabric all down the years. Yesterday in conversation, I was using "The Mill." Robinson could make lyric talk like drama. What imagination for speech in "John Gorham"! He is at his height between quotation marks.

> The miller's wife had waited long,
>   The tea was cold, the fire was dead;
> And there might yet be nothing wrong
>   In how he went and what he said:
> "There are no millers any more,"
>   Was all that she had heard him say.

"There are no millers any more." It might be an edict of some power against industrialism. But no, it is of wider application. It is a sinister jest at the expense of all investors of life or capital. The market shifts and leaves them with a car-barn full of dead trolley cars. At twenty I commit myself to a life of religion. Now, if religion should go out of fashion in twenty-five years, there would I be, forty-five years old, unfitted for anything else and too old to learn anything else. It seems immoral to have to bet on such high things as lives of art, business, or the church. But in effect, we have no alternative. None but an all-wise and all-powerful government could take the responsibility of keeping us out of the gamble or of insuring us against loss once we were in.

The guarded pathos of "Mr. Flood's Party" is what makes it

merciless. We are to bear in mind the number of moons listening.
Two, as on the planet Mars. No less. No more ("No more, sir; that
will do"). One moon (albeit a moon, no sun) would have laid grief
too bare. More than two would have dissipated grief entirely and
would have amounted to dissipation. The emotion had to be held
at a point.

> He set the jug down slowly at his feet
> With trembling care, knowing that most things break;
> And only when assured that on firm earth
> It stood, as the uncertain lives of men
> Assuredly did not . . .

There twice it gleams. Nor is it lost even where it is perhaps lost
sight of in the dazzle of all those golden girls at the end of "The
Sheaves." Granted a few fair days in a world where not all days are
fair.

> "Well, Mr. Flood, we have the harvest moon
> Again, and we may not have many more;
> The bird is on the wing, the poet says,
> And you and I have said it here before.
> Drink to the bird."

Poetry transcends itself in the playfulness of the toast.

Robinson has gone to his place in American literature and left
his human place among us vacant. We mourn, but with the qualification that, after all, his life was a revel in the felicities of language.
And not just to no purpose. None has deplored

> The inscrutable profusion of the Lord
> Who shaped as one of us a thing

so sad and at the same time so happy in achievement. Not for me
to search his sadness to its source. He knew how to forbid en-
croachment. And there is solid satisfaction in a sadness that is not
just a fishing for ministration and consolation. Give us immedicable
woes—woes that nothing can be done for—woes flat and final. And
then to play. The play's the thing. Play's the thing. All virtue in
"as if."

<pre>
                   As if the last of days
        Were fading and all wars were done.
</pre>

As if they were. As if, as if!

THE FIGURE A POEM MAKES

This was Frost's favorite preface. He wrote it in 1939 for the first and succeeding editions of his collected poems. It contains his most famous and lyrical description of the act of poetic creation.

Abstraction is an old story with the philosophers, but it has been like a new toy in the hands of the artists of our day. Why can't we have any one quality of poetry we choose by itself? We can have in thought. Then it will go hard if we can't in practice. Our lives for it.

Granted no one but a humanist much cares how sound a poem is if it is only *a* sound. The sound is the gold in the ore. Then we will have the sound out alone and dispense with the inessential. We do till we make the discovery that the object in writing poetry is to make all poems sound as different as possible from each other, and the resources for that of vowels, consonants, punctuation, syntax, words, sentences, meter are not enough. We need the help of context—meaning—subject matter. That is the greatest help towards variety. All that can be done with words is soon told. So also with meters—particularly in our language where there are virtually but two, strict iambic and loose iambic. The ancients with many were still poor if they depended on meters for all tune. It is painful to watch our sprung-rhythmists straining at the point of omitting one short from a foot for relief from monotony. The possibilities for tune from the dramatic tones of meaning struck across the rigidity of a limited meter are endless. And we are back in poetry as merely one more art of having something to say, sound or unsound. Probably better if sound, because deeper and from wider experience.

Then there is this wildness whereof it is spoken. Granted again that it has an equal claim with sound to being a poem's better half. If it is a wild tune, it is a poem. Our problem then is, as modern abstractionists, to have the wildness pure; to be wild with nothing to be wild about. We bring up as aberrationists, giving way to undirected associations and kicking ourselves from one chance suggestion to another in all directions as of a hot afternoon in the life of a grasshopper. Theme alone can steady us down. Just as the first mystery was how a poem could have a tune in such a straightness as meter, so the second mystery is how a poem can have wildness and at the same time a subject that shall be fulfilled.

It should be of the pleasure of a poem itself to tell how it can. The figure a poem makes. It begins in delight and ends in wisdom. The figure is the same as for love. No one can really hold that the ecstasy should be static and stand still in one place. It begins in delight, it inclines to the impulse, it assumes direction with the first line laid down, it runs a course of lucky events, and ends in a clarification of life—not necessarily a great clarification, such as sects and cults are founded on, but in a momentary stay against confusion. It has denouement. It has an outcome that though unforeseen was predestined from the first image of the original mood —and indeed from the very mood. It is but a trick poem and no poem at all if the best of it was thought of first and saved for the last. It finds its own name as it goes and discovers the best waiting for it in some final phrase at once wise and sad—the happy-sad blend of the drinking song.

No tears in the writer, no tears in the reader. No surprise for the writer, no surprise for the reader. For me the initial delight is in the surprise of remembering something I didn't know I knew. I am in a place, in a situation, as if I had materialized from cloud or risen out of the ground. There is a glad recognition of the long lost and the rest follows. Step by step the wonder of unexpected supply keeps growing. The impressions most useful to my purpose seem always those I was unaware of and so made no note of at the time when taken, and the conclusion is come to that like giants we are always hurling experience ahead of us to pave the future with against the day when we may want to strike a line of purpose across it for somewhere. The line will have the more charm for not being mechanically straight. We enjoy the straight crookedness of a good walking stick. Modern instruments of precision are being used to make things crooked as if by eye and hand in the old days.

I tell how there may be a better wildness of logic than of inconsequence. But the logic is backward, in retrospect, after the act. It must be more felt than seen ahead like prophecy. It must be a revelation, or a series of revelations, as much for the poet as for the reader. For it to be that there must have been the greatest freedom of the material to move about in it and to establish relations in it regardless of time and space, previous relation, and everything but affinity. We prate of freedom. We call our schools free because we are not free to stay away from them till we are sixteen years of age. I have given up my democratic prejudices and now willingly set the lower classes free to be completely taken care of by the upper classes. Political freedom is nothing to me. I bestow it right and left. All I would keep for myself is the freedom of my material—the condition of body and mind now and then to summons aptly from the vast chaos of all I have lived through.

Scholars and artists thrown together are often annoyed at the puzzle of where they differ. Both work for knowledge; but I suspect they differ most importantly in the way their knowledge is come by. Scholars get theirs with conscientious thoroughness along projected lines of logic; poets theirs cavalierly and as it happens in and out of books. They stick to nothing deliberately, but let what will stick to them like burrs where they walk in the fields. No acquirement is on assignment, or even self-assignment. Knowledge of the second kind is much more available in the wild free ways of wit and art. A school boy may be defined as one who can tell you what he knows in the order in which he learned it. The artist must value himself as he snatches a thing from some previous order in time and space into a new order with not so much as a ligature clinging to it of the old place where it was organic.

More than once I should have lost my soul to radicalism if it had been the originality it was mistaken for by its young converts. Originality and initiative are what I ask for my country. For myself the originality need be no more than the freshness of a poem run in the way I have described: from delight to wisdom. The figure is the same as for love. Like a piece of ice on a hot stove the poem must ride on its own melting. A poem may be worked over once it is in being, but may not be worried into being. Its most precious quality will remain its having run itself and carried away the poet with it. Read it a hundred times: it will forever keep its freshness as a metal keeps its fragrance. It can never lose its sense of a meaning that once unfolded by surprise as it went.

THE CONSTANT SYMBOL

Through all the posturing of the prose here, Frost expounds his almost existential concept of the way a poem transcends its original idea and creates itself through the very struggle with the discipline of form. Used as the preface to the 1946 Modern Library edition of Frost's poems, it was first published separately in the Atlantic Monthly *of October, 1946.*

There seems to be some such folk saying as that easy to understand is contemptible, hard to understand irritating. The implication is that just easy enough, just hard enough, right in the middle, is what literary criticism ought to foster. A glance backward over the past convinces me otherwise. The *Iliad, Odyssey*, and *Aeneid* are easy. The *Purgatorio* is said to be hard. The Song of Songs *is* hard. There have been works lately to surpass all records for hardness. Some knotted riddles tell what may be worth our trouble. But hard or easy seems to me of slight use as a test either way.

Texture is surely something. A good piece of weaving takes rank with a picture as decoration for the wall of a studio, though it must be admitted to verge on the arty. There is a time of apprenticeship to texture when it shouldn't matter if the stuff is never made up into anything. There may be scraps of repeated form all over it. But form as a whole! Don't be shocking! The title of his first book was *Fragments*. The artist has to grow up and coarsen a little before he looks on texture as not an end in itself.

There are many other things I have found myself saying about poetry, but the chiefest of these is that it is metaphor, saying one thing and meaning another, saying one thing in terms of another, the pleasure of ulteriority. Poetry is simply made of metaphor. So also is philosophy—and science, too, for that matter, if it will take the soft impeachment from a friend. Every poem is a new metaphor inside or it is nothing. And there is a sense in which all poems are the same old metaphor always.

Every single poem written regular is a symbol small or great of the way the will has to pitch into commitments deeper and deeper to a rounded conclusion and then be judged for whether any original intention it had has been strongly spent or weakly lost; be it in art, politics, school, church, business, love, or marriage—in a piece of work or in a career. Strongly spent is synonymous with kept.

We may speak after sentence, resenting judgment. How can the world know anything so intimate as what we were intending to do? The answer is the world presumes to know. The ruling passion in man is not as Viennese as is claimed. It is rather a gregarious instinct to keep together by minding each other's business. Grex rather than sex. We *must* be preserved from becoming egregious. The beauty of socialism is that it will end the individuality that is always crying out mind your own business. Terence's answer would be all human business is my business. No more invisible means of support, no more invisible motives, no more invisible anything. The ultimate commitment is giving in to it that an outsider may see what we were up to sooner and better than we ourselves. The bard has said in effect, Unto these forms did I commend the spirit. It may take him a year after the act to confess he only betrayed the spirit with a rhymster's cleverness and to forgive his enemies the critics for not having listened to his oaths and protestations to the contrary. Had he anything to be true to? Was he true to it? Did he use good words? You couldn't tell unless you made out what idea they were supposed to be good for. Every poem is an epitome of the great predicament; a figure of the will braving alien entanglements.

Take the President in the White House. A study of the success of his intention might have to go clear back to when as a young politician, youthfully step-careless, he made the choice between the two parties of our system. He may have stood for a moment wishing he knew of a third party nearer the ideal; but only for a moment, since he was practical. And in fact he may have been so little impressed with the importance of his choice that he left his first commitment to be made for him by his friends and relatives. It was only a small commitment anyway, like a kiss. He can scarcely remember how much credit he deserved personally for the decision it took. Calculation is usually no part in the first step in any walk. And behold him now a statesman so multifariously closed in on with obligations and answerabilities that sometimes he loses his august temper. He might as well have got himself into a sestina royal.

Or he may be a religious nature who lightly gets committed to a nameable church through an older friend in plays and games at the Y.M.C.A. The next he knows he is in a theological school and next in the pulpit of a Sunday wrestling with the angel for a blessing on his self-defensive interpretation of the Creed. What of his original intention now? At least he has had the advantage of having it more in his heart than in his head; so that he should have made shift to assert it without being chargeable with compromise. He could go a long way before he had to declare anything he could be held to. He began with freedom to squander. He has to acknowledge himself in a tighter and tighter place. But his courage asked for it. It would have been the same if he had gone to the North Pole or climbed Everest. All that concerns *us* is whether his story was one of conformance or performance.

There's an indulgent smile I get for the recklessness of the unnecessary commitment I made when I came to the first line in the second stanza of a poem in this book called "Stopping by Woods on a Snowy Evening." I was riding too high to care what trouble I incurred. And it was all right so long as I didn't suffer deflection.

The poet goes in like a rope skipper to make the most of his opportunities. If he trips himself he stops the rope. He is of our stock and has been brought up by ear to choice of two metres, strict iambic and loose iambic (not to count varieties of the latter).

He may have any length of line up to six feet. He may use an assortment of line lengths for any shape of stanza like Herrick in "To Daffodils." Not that he is running wild. His intention is of course a particular mood that won't be satisfied with anything less than its own fulfillment. But it is not yet a thought concerned with what becomes it. One thing to know it by: it shrinks shyly from anticipatory expression. Tell love beforehand and, as Blake says, it loses flow without filling the mould; the cast will be a reject. The freshness of a poem belongs absolutely to its not having been thought out and then set to verse as the verse in turn might be set to music. A poem is the emotion of having a thought while the reader waits a little anxiously for the success of dawn. The only discipline to begin with is the inner mood that at worst may give the poet a false start or two like the almost microscopic filament of cotton that goes before the blunt thread-end and must be picked up first by the eye of the needle. He must be entranced to the exact premonition. No mystery is meant. When familiar friends approach each other in the street both are apt to have this experience in feeling before knowing the pleasantry they will inflict on each other in passing.

Probably there is something between the mood and the vocal imagination (images of the voice speaking) that determines a man's first commitment to metre and length of line.

Suppose him to have written down "When in disgrace with Fortune and men's eyes." He has uttered about as much as he has to live up to in the theme as in the form. Odd how the two advance into the open pari passu. He has given out that he will descend into Hades, but he has confided in no one how far before he will turn back, or whether he will turn back at all, and by what jutting points of rock he will pick his way. He may proceed as in blank verse. Two lines more, however, and he has let himself in for rhyme, three more and he has set himself a stanza. Up to this point his discipline has been the self-discipline whereof it is written in so great praise. The harsher discipline from without is now well begun. He who knows not both knows neither. His wordly commitments are now three or four deep. Between us, he was no doubt bent on the sonnet in the first place from habit, and what's the use in pretending he was a freer agent than he had any ambition to be? He had made most of his commitments all in one plunge. The only suspense he asks us to share with him is in the theme. He goes down, for instance, to a depth that must surprise him as much as it does us. But he doesn't even have the say of how long his piece will be. Any worry is as to whether he will outlast or last out the fourteen lines—have to cramp or stretch to come out even—have enough bread for the butter or butter for the bread. As a matter of fact, he gets through in twelve lines and doesn't know quite what to do with the last two.

Things like that and worse are the reason the sonnet is so suspect a form and has driven so many to free verse and even to the novel. Many a quatrain is salvaged from a sonnet that went agley. Dobson confesses frankly to having changed from one form to another after starting: "I intended an Ode and it turned to a Sonnet." But he reverses the usual order of being driven from the harder down to the easier. And he has a better excuse for weakness of will than most, namely, Rose.

Jeremiah, it seems, has had his sincerity questioned because the anguish of his lamentations was tamable to the form of twenty-two stanzas for the twenty-two letters of the alphabet. The Hebrew alphabet has been kept to the twenty-two letters it came out of Egypt with, so the number twenty-two means as much form as ever.

But there they go again with the old doubt about law and order. (The communist looks forward to a day of order without law, bless his merciful heart.) To the right person it must seem naive to distrust form as such. The very words of the dictionary are a restriction to make the best of or stay out of and be silent. Coining new words isn't encouraged. We play the words as we find them. We make them do. Form in language is such a disjected lot of old broken pieces it seems almost as non-existent as the spirit till the two embrace in the sky. They are not to be thought of as encountering in rivalry but in creation. No judgment on either alone counts. We see what Whitman's extravagance may have meant when he said the body was the soul.

Here is where it all comes out. The mind is a baby giant who, more provident in the cradle than he knows, has hurled his paths in life all round ahead of him like playthings given—data so-called. They are vocabulary, grammar, prosody, and diary, and it will go hard if he can't find stepping stones of them for his feet wherever he wants to go. The way will be zigzag, but it will be a straight crookedness like the walking stick he cuts himself in the bushes for an emblem. He will be judged as he does or doesn't let this zig or that zag project him off out of his general direction.

Teacher or student or investigator whose chance on these defenseless lines may seize, your pardon if for once I point you out what ordinarily you would point me out. To some it will seem strange that I have written my verse regular all this time without knowing till yesterday that it was from fascination with this constant symbol I celebrate. To the right person it will seem lucky; since in finding out too much too soon there is danger of arrest. Does anyone believe I would have committed myself to the treason-reason-season rhyme-set in my "Reluctance" if I had been blasé enough to know that these three words about exhausted the possibilities? No rhyming dictionary for me to make me face the facts of rhyme. I may say the strain of rhyming is less since I came to see words as phrase-ends to countless phrases just as the syllables ly, ing, and ation are word-ends to countless words. Leave something to learn later. We'd have lost most of our innocence by forty anyway even if we never went to school a day.

Reviews

THE POETRY OF AMY LOWELL

Frost's attitude toward Amy Lowell passed from initial dependence and a qualified sense of awe, through condescension and mockery, to a more active dislike. This review which appraises her poetic stature, written shortly after her death and first published in the Christian Science Monitor *of May 16, 1925, reveals an admirable capacity to separate the personal from the professional in Frost's critical judgment. It is not unqualified praise, yet it is one of the most positive and relevant summaries of Miss Lowell's achievement ever written.*

It is absurd to think that the only way to tell if a poem is lasting is to wait and see if it lasts. The right reader of a good poem can tell the moment it strikes him that he has taken an immortal wound —that he will never get over it. That is to say, permanence in poetry as in love is perceived instantly. It hasn't to await the test of time. The proof of a poem is not that we have never forgotten it, but that we knew at sight that we never could forget it. There was a barb to it and a tocsin that we owned to at once. How often I have heard it in the voice and seen it in the eyes of this generation that Amy Lowell had lodged poetry with them to stay.

The most exciting movement in nature is not progress, advance, but expansion and contraction, the opening and shutting of the eye, the hand, the heart, the mind. We throw our arms wide with a gesture of religion to the universe; we close them around a person. We explore and adventure for a while and then we draw in to consolidate our gains. The breathless swing is between subject matter and form. Amy Lowell was distinguished in a period of dilation when poetry, in the effort to include a larger material, stretched itself almost to the breaking of the verse. Little ones with no more apparatus than a tea-cup looked on with alarm. She helped make it stirring times for a decade to those immediately concerned with art and to many not so immediately.

The water in our eyes from her poetry is not warm with any suspicion of tears; it is water flung cold, bright and many-colored from flowers gathered in her formal garden in the morning. Her Imagism lay chiefly in images to the eye. She flung flowers and everything there. Her poetry was forever a clear resonant calling off of things seen.

THE PREREQUISITES

This essay first appeared in the New York Times Book Review *for March 21, 1954, and was later used as the preface to Frost's 1954 volume* Aforesaid. *Though it seems at first a curious choice for an introduction to his own poetry, Frost is perhaps suggesting that his own critical approach here—the assumption that life itself provides the prerequisites to a proper understanding of a poem—is a valuable one for any poetry.*

Some sixty years ago a young reader ran into serious trouble with the blind last stanza of a poem otherwise perfectly intelligible. The interest today might be in what he then did about it. He simply left it to shift for itself. He might see to it if he ever saw it again. He guessed he was no more anxious to understand the poem than the poem was to be understood.

He might have gone to college for help. But he had just left college to improve his mind if he had any. Or he might have gone to Asia. The whole poem smacked of Asia. He suspected a whole religion behind it different from the one he was brought up to. But as he was no traveler except on foot he must have gone by way of the Bering Strait when frozen over and that might have taken him an epoch from East to West as it had the Indians from West to East.

The poem was called "Brahma" and he was lilting along on such lines as the following in easy recognition:

> They reckon ill who leave me out
> When me they fly I am the wings.

I am the doubter and the doubt
And I the hymn the Brahmin sings.

which was all very pretty. For Brahma he naturally read God—
not the God of the Old Testament nor of the New either, but
near enough. Though no special liberal he valued himself on his
tolerance of heresy in great thinkers. He could always lend himself to an unsound idea for the duration of the piece and had been
even heard to wish people would cling to their heresies long
enough for him to go and tell on them.

Success in taking figures of speech is as intoxicating as success
in making figures of speech. It had to be just when he was flushed
with having held his own with the poem so far and was thinking
"good easy man" "What a good boy am I" that the disaster happened. The words were still Brahma's:

The strong gods pine for my abode
And pine in vain the sacred seven
But thou meek lover of the good
Find me and turn thy back on Heaven.

There he blacked out as if he had bumped his head and he only
came to dazed. I remember his anger in asking if anybody had a
right to talk like that. But he wasn't as put out as he let on to be.
He didn't go back on poetry for more than the particular poem
or on that for more than the time being. His subconscious intention was to return on it by stealth some day if only it would stay
in print till he was ready for it. All was he didn't want the wrong
kind of help. The heart sinks when robbed of the chance to see
for itself what a poem is all about. Any immediate preface is like
cramming the night before an examination. Too late, too late!
Any footnote while the poem is going is too late. Any subsequent
explanation is as dispiriting as the explanation of a joke. Being
taught poems reduces them to the rank of mere information. He
was sure the Muse would thank him for reserving a few of her
best for being achieved on the spur of the moment.

Approach to the poem must be from afar off, even generations off. He should close in on it on converging lines from many directions like the divisions of an army upon a battlefield.

A poem is best read in the light of all the other poems ever written. We read A the better to read B (we have to start somewhere; we may get very little out of A). We read B the better to read C, C the better to read D, D the better to go back and get something more out of A. Progress is not the aim, but circulation. The thing is to get among the poems where they hold each other apart in their places as the stars do.

And if he stubbornly stayed away from college and Asia (he hated to be caught at his age grooming his brains in public) perhaps in time college and Asia, even the Taj Mahal, might come to him with the prerequisites to that poem and to much else not yet clear.

Well, it so happened. For the story has a happy ending. Not fifty years later when the poem turned up again he found himself in a position to deal with all but two lines of it. He was not quite satisfied that the reference to "strong gods," plural, was fair poetry practice. Were these Titans or Yidags or, perish the thought, Olympians?—Oh no! not Olympians. But he now saw through the "meek lover of the good" who sounded so deceptively Christian. His meekness must have meant the perfect detachment from ambition and desire that can alone rescue us from the round of existence. And the "me" worth turning "thy back on Heaven" for must of course be Nirvana—the only nothing that is something. He had grown very fastidious about not calling the round of existence a wheel. He was a confirmed symbolist.

Lectures

LECTURE TO THE BROWNE AND NICHOLS SCHOOL, 1915

These notes from a lecture that Frost gave at the Browne and Nichols School on May 10, 1915, were transcribed by George Browne. They provide a rare glimpse of Frost analyzing one of his own poems, and reveal clearly his preoccupation with the speaking voice.

Mr. Browne has alluded to the seeing eye. I want to call your attention to the function of the imagining ear. Your attention is too often called to the poet with extraordinarily vivid sight, and with the faculty of choosing exceptionally telling words for the sight. But equally valuable, even for schoolboy themes, is the use of the ear for material for compositions. When you listen to a speaker, you hear words, to be sure,—but you also hear tones. The problem is to note them, to imagine them again, and to get them down in writing. But few of you probably ever thought of the possibility or of the necessity of doing this. You are generally told to distinguish simple, compound, and complex sentences,—long and short, —periodic and loose,—to varying sentence structure, etc. "Not all sentences are short, like those of Emerson, the writer of the best American prose. You must vary your sentences, like Stevenson, etc." All this is missing the vital element. I always had a dream of getting away from it, when I was teaching school,—and, in my own writing and teaching, of bringing in the *living* sounds of speech. For it is a fundamental fact that certain forms depend on the sound;—e.g., note the various tones of irony, acquiescence, doubt, etc. in the farmer's "I guess so." And the great problem is, can you get these tones down on paper? How *do* you tell the tone? By the context, by the animating spirit of the living voice. And how many tones do you think there are flying round? Hundreds of them—hundreds never brought to book. Compare T. E. Brown's *To a Blackbird:* "O blackbird, what a boy you are"

142

Compare W. B. Yeats's "Who dreamed that beauty passes like a dream"

I went to church, once (loud laughter)—this will sound funnier when I tell you that the only thing I remember is the long line of "Nows" that I counted. The repetition grew tiresome. I knew just when to expect a 'Now', and I knew beforehand just what the tone was going to be. There is no objection to repetition of the right kind,—only to the mechanical repetition of the tone. It is all right to repeat, if there is something for the voice to do. The vital thing, then, to consider in all composition, in prose or verse, is the ACTION of the voice,—sound-posturing, gesture. Get the *stuff* of life into the technique of your writing. That's the only escape from dry rhetoric.

When I began to teach, and long after I began to write, I didn't know what the matter was with me and my writing and with other people's writing. I recall distinctly the joy with which I had the first satisfaction of getting an expression adequate for my thought. I was so delighted that I had to cry. It was the second stanza of the little poem on the Butterfly, written in my eighteenth year. And the Sound in the mouths of men I found to be the basis of all effective expression,—not merely words or phrases, but sentences,—living things flying round,—the vital parts of speech. And my poems are to be read in the appreciative tones of this live speech. For example, there are five tones in this first stanza,

The Pasture

I'm going out to clean the pasture spring;   (light, informing tone)

I'll only stop to rake the leaves away   ("only" tone—reservation)

(And wait to watch the water clear, I may):   (supplementary, possibility)

I sha'n't be gone long.—You come too.   (free tone, assuring)

(after thought, inviting)

"Rather well for me"—

I'm going out to fetch the little calf   (Similar, free, per-
That's standing by the mother. It's so young,   suasive, assuring,
It totters when she licks it with her tongue.   and inviting
I sha'n't be gone long.—You come too.   tones in second
                                                                        stanza)

(Similar demonstration in "Mending Wall". . . .) Just see and
hear the two farmers across the old wall in the spring, picking up
stones, and placing them back in their places on the wall. Note
the tone, challenging and threatening, at

> "We have to use a spell to make them balance:
> " 'Stay where you are until our backs are turned!' "

Playful note at "Oh, just another kind of outdoor game"—
Idiomatic balance, "He is all pine and I am apple orchard."
Incredulity of the other's dictum: "Good fences make good
neighbors." and "But here there are no cows." Shaking his head
as he says, "Before I built a wall" etc.—Can't you see him? and
hear him?

So, my advice to you boys in all your composition work is:
"Gather your sentences by ear, and reimagine them in your
writing." [. . .]

THE UNMADE WORD, OR
FETCHING AND FAR-FETCHING

*Frost gave another talk to the boys of the Browne and Nichols
School on 13 March 1918, and once more George Browne transcribed
it. The points are oversimplified and the tone somewhat condescend-
ing—perhaps the class was younger than in the 1915 lecture—but the
concepts and terminology are important ones in Frost's critical thinking. The clarity of their presentation demonstrates why he was so
successful as a teacher.*

There are two ways of taking notes: when a man is speaking to you and after he has spoken to you. I never could take notes while a man was talking; but I have known men who have taken notes that way successfully. I am going to talk to you this morning, briefly, and I want you to try to take the thing in as a whole; then write it up for me afterward as a reporter would write an account for his paper—with no glowing introduction, but just the mere, honest, straightforward report of what I say to you.

I am going to call the thing by a name, two names in fact. You needn't pay much attention to them at first, and I will repeat them at the end when perhaps you will understand them better. I will call it first "the unmade word," or second, "Fetching and Far-fetching." You won't know much about either: I couldn't give you those names as theme subjects. Probably you don't know what I mean; I shouldn't have to talk to you if you did.

There are two kinds of language: the spoken language and the written language—our everyday speech which we call the vernacular; and a more literary, sophisticated, artificial, elegant language that belongs to books. We often hear it said that a man talks like a book in this second way. We object to anybody's talking in this literary, artificial English; we don't object to anybody's writing in it; we rather expect people to write in a literary, somewhat artificial style. I, myself, could get along very well without this bookish language altogether. I agree with the poet who visited this country not long ago when he said that all our literature has got to come down, sooner or later, to the talk of everyday life. William Butler Yeats says that all our words, phrases, and idioms to be effective must be in the manner of everyday speech.

We've got to come down to this speech of everyday, to begin with—the hard everyday word of the street, business, trades, work in summer—to begin with; but there is some sort of obligation laid on us, to lift the words of every day, to give them a metaphorical turn. No, you don't want to use that term—give the words a poetic touch. I'll show you what I mean by an example: take for example the word "lemon," that's a good practical word with no literary associations—a word that you use with the grocer and in the kitchen; it has no literary associations at all; "Peach" is another one; but you boys have taken these two words and given them a poetic twist, a poetic movement—you have not left the peach on the tree or in the basket; you couldn't let the lemon alone, you had to move it. What is the need in you of moving words? Take the word "pill" (laughter)—have you let that alone? A person is a pill, a baseball is a pill. You sometimes move even phrases. In baseball you have the phrase, "put one over on him." I suppose I know the origin of that phrase, though it's not one of my invention. Doesn't it mean "pitch one by him that he doesn't hit at at all." Isn't that what it means? Correct me if I'm wrong. "Get his goat" has been explained to me, but I didn't like the explanation. I don't know the origin of that phrase. Now the rest of the world—ladies that never saw a baseball game in their lives, who couldn't trace to their origin any of these phrases—are now using these words and phrases as a matter of everyday speech. Poetry and literature are plumb full, chock full of words and phrases like "lemon, peach, pill, and put one over on him."

But are such expressions allowable in writing? No. When a man sits down with pen and paper to write, he declares his purpose of being original, instead of taking these second-hand words and phrases. I am sick of people who use only these ready-made words and phrases. I like better a boy who invents them for himself—who takes a word or phrase from where it lies and moves it to another place. Did you ever get one up? Are you contented to use the same old words all the time or do you ever get up a new one? Now "fetching" a word or name from its place is what your textbooks call using words figuratively—metaphor, simile, analogy, or allegory —equivalent to using the word "like"; "like a peach"; he isn't a lemon, but "like a lemon." The other day someone said the snow was "mealy." I liked the word. It sounded fresh; but it was an old one that I had heard in the country, and it had lost some of its goodness from use. The other day I heard a new morning salutation; instead of "how d'y'do, how are things coming?"—a new one anyway—a man came into a train and said, "Are you satisfied?" Ever hear that? Is that a going one? At any rate the man had an inspiration and got a new one that pleased me—as if they had had a little quarrel and one wanted to know if the other was satisfied. He had "fetched" the phrase from its regular place to a new and effective place, and got away with it.

He didn't try to be original; but I know people who like that sort of thing so well that they are forever "fetching" words and phrases too far. They overdo it. Well, I don't see why a fellow shouldn't overdo it, at the beginning—it's freshening his language. "How d'y, how do you do, how are you?"—we are tired of those expressions, they need freshening. Now, there are two ways of freshening your language. First by "fetching" words out of their places, and second by going to a thesaurus [a commotion]. You don't know what a thesaurus is? Well, it's a dictionary of synonyms —ministers use 'em, poor men! After they've preached a long time in one place they begin to suspect that their parishioners are getting a little tired of their vocabulary, so they freshen their sermons out of a dictionary. But what I have chiefly in mind is a figurative fetching of fresh words to your use. The word lies in our everyday speech, practical, hard, and unliterary; and that's the way I like the word— there's where my fun with it begins. I don't care for the word already made figurative. I haven't done anything to it. I don't see what more can be done to it. Mr. Browne doesn't object to my poking a little fun at him. He tells me that yesterday morning, inspired by the brilliant effect of the ice encased trees, reflecting the morning in prismatic colors, he strove to add a new word to your vocabulary by quoting the opening sentence of Emerson's famous Divinity School Address: "In this *refulgent* summer it has been a luxury to draw the breath of life." Of course, anybody would sit up and take notice when a speaker began like that. Undoubtedly there's a freshness there in the use of that word that amounts to brilliance; but you ought not to use the word in just that way. Emerson made it his own; let it alone.

But do the same thing with *your* new words. Compare the use of the word "alien," a practical, everyday word with whose meaning you are familiar—a common word until a great poet, Keats, used it in his "Ode to the Nightingale"

> "The self-same song that found a path
> Through the sad heart of Ruth, when, sick for home,
> She stood in tears amid the alien corn"

That use of "alien" fascinated poets as "peach" and "lemon" fascinate you boys. All poets are now using "alien." I've heard of "alien bean." The idea now is, use it anywhere where you want to be poetic, as you use "peach, lemon, pill," etc., when you want to sound like a boy—slangy, fresh. [. . .]

Now I'm going to read you, at Mr. Browne's request, one of my poems, and I'd like to point out to you one or two of these words that I "fetched"—and I'd like you to consider where I got them, where I fetched them to, and whether I fetched them too far. In this poem on "The Birches," I'm trying to give you the effect of a similar ice storm; the birch twigs encased in ice:

> "Often you must have seen them
> Loaded with ice a sunny winter morning
> After a rain. They click upon themselves
> As the breeze rises, and turn many-colored
> As the stir cracks and crazes their enamel."

There are other words in the poem I like, but where do you think I got that word "crazes"? [no answer] Mr. Frost went to the blackboard, and drew the pattern of crackly china, like the Dedham pottery.

> "Such heaps of broken glass to sweep away
> You'd think the inner dome of heaven had fallen."

I wonder if you think I fetched that word dome too far? It's not so good as the other, in spite of the "broken glass," but I like it. [. . .]

·

Interviews

ROBERT FROST, NEW AMERICAN POET

As part of Frost's self-publicizing campaign when he returned to the United States, he sought out the support of Amy Lowell and the critic and anthologist William Stanley Braithwaite, both of whom carried critical weight in Boston. This interview by Braithwaite was originally published in the Boston Evening Transcript *for May 8, 1915.*

The success which has immediately come to the poetry of Robert Frost is unique. It has no exact parallel in the experience of the art in this country during the present generation. [. . .]

To appreciate Mr. Frost's poetry perfectly one has got to regard carefully the two backgrounds from which it is projected; fully under the influence of his art these two backgrounds merge into one, though each has its special distinction. There is the background of his material, the environment and character which belong to a special community; and there is the background of art in which the fidelity of speech is artistically brought into literature. This latter is a practice that brings up large and important questions of language and meaning in relation to life on the one hand and to literature on the other.

Mr. Frost has been through the longest period of experimentation in mastering the technique of his art of any other American poet. What he finally arrived at in poetic expression he finds as the highest accomplishment in the greatest English poets and asserts that the American poets who have shown unquestionable genius, especially a man like Edwin Arlington Robinson, have in a large measure the same quality of speech which is at once both artistic and the literal tone of human talk. But no poet in either England or America, except this newly arrived New England poet, has consciously developed and practiced this essential and vital quality of poetry which he characterizes as sound-posturing.

The poet was in his twentieth year when he realized that the speech of books and the speech of life were far more fundamentally different than was supposed. His models up to this period, as with all youthful poets and writers, had been literary models. But he found quite by accident that real artistic speech was only to be copied from life. On his New Hampshire farm he discovered this in the character of a man with whom he used to drive along the country roads. Having discovered this speech he set about copying it in poetry, getting the principles down by rigorous observation and reproduction through the long years which intervened to the publication of his books.

He also discovered that where English poetry was greatest it was by virtue of this same method in the poet, and, as I shall show, in his talk with me he illustrated it in Shakespeare, Shelley, Wordsworth, and Emerson. That these poets did not formulate the principles by which they obtained these subtle artistic effects, but accomplished it wholly unconscious of its exact importance, he also suggested. But with a deliberate recognition of it as a poetic value in the poets to come, he sees an entirely new development in the art of verse.

The invitation which brought Mr. Frost to Boston to read the Phi Beta Kappa poem on Wednesday at Tufts College gave me the opportunity to get from the poet his views on the principles of sound-posturing in verse and some reflections on contemporary poets and poetry in England and America.

Before returning home, it will be interesting to note, the publication of Mr. Frost's books in England awakened a critical sympathy and acceptance, among English writers, of his ideas. His work won over, by its sheer poetic achievement, critics and poets, who had not realized before the possibilities of reproducing the exact tone of meaning in human speech in literary form. Where the poet's work is not fully appreciated in this country is where this principle is not understood. The substance of New England farm life of which his poetry is made has attracted immense interest, but in some quarters the appreciation of this substance is a little modified because the reader has only partially grasped the significance of the form. So it was this I wished the poet to explain in my very first question.

"First," he said, "let me find a name for this principle which will convey to the mind what I mean by this effect which I try to put into my poetry. And secondly, do not let your readers be deceived that this is anything new. Before I give you the details in proof of its importance, in fact of its essential place in the writing of the highest poetry, let me quote these lines from Emerson's 'Monadnoc,' where, in almost a particular manner, he sets forth unmistakably what I mean:

> Now in sordid weeds they sleep,
> In dulness now their secret keep;
> Yet, will you learn our ancient speech,
> These the masters who can teach.
> Fourscore or a hundred words
> All their vocal muse affords;
> But they turn them in a fashion
> Past clerks' or statesmen's art or passion.
> I can spare the college bell,
> And the learned lecture, well;
> Spare the clergy and libraries,
> Institutes and dictionaries,
> For that hearty English root
> Thrives here, unvalued, underfoot.
> Rude poets of the tavern hearth,
> Squandering your unquoted mirth,
> Which keeps the ground and never soars,
> While Jake retorts and Reuben roars;
> Scoff of yeoman strong and stark,
> Goes like bullet to its mark;
> While the solid curse and jeer
> Never balk the waiting ear.

"Understand these lines perfectly and you will understand what I mean when I call this principle 'sound-posturing' or, more literally, getting the sound of sense.

"What we do get in life and miss so often in literature is the sentence sounds that underlie the words. Words in themselves do not convey meaning, and to [. . . prove] this, which may seem entirely unreasonable to any one who does not understand the psychology of sound, let us take the example of two people who are talking on the other side of a closed door, whose voices can be heard but whose words cannot be distinguished. Even though the words do not carry, the sound of them does, and the listener can catch the meaning of the conversation. This is because every meaning has a particular sound-posture; or, to put it in another way, the sense of every meaning has a particular sound which each individual is instinctively familiar with and without at all being conscious of the exact words that are being used is able to understand the thought, idea, or emotion that is being conveyed.

"What I am most interested in emphasizing in the application of this belief to art is the sentence of sound, because to me a sentence is not interesting merely in conveying a meaning of words. It must do something more; it must convey a meaning by sound."

"But," I queried, "do you not come into conflict with metrical sounds to which the laws of poetry conform in creating rhythm?"

"No," the poet replied, "because you must understand this sound of which I speak has principally to do with tone. It is what Mr. Bridges, the Poet Laureate, characterized as speech-rhythm. Meter has to do with beat, and sound-posture has a definite relation as an alternate tone between the beats. The two are one in creation but separate in analysis.

"If we go back far enough we will discover the sound of sense existed before words, that something in the voice or vocal gesture made primitive man convey a meaning to his fellow before the race developed a more elaborate and concrete symbol of communication in language. I have even read that our American Indians possessed, besides a picture-language, a means of communication (though it was not said how far it was developed) by the sound of sense. And what is this but calling up with the imagination, and recognizing, the images of sound?

"When Wordsworth said, 'Write with your eye on the object,' or (in another sense) it was important to visualize, he really meant something more. That something carries out what I mean by writing with your ear to the voice.

"This is what Wordsworth did himself in all his best poetry, proving that there can be no creative imagination unless there is a summoning up of experience, fresh from life, which has not hitherto been evoked. The power, however, to do this does not last very long in the life of a poet. After ten years Wordsworth had very nearly exhausted his, giving us only flashes of it now and then. As language only really exists in the mouths of men, here again Wordsworth was right in trying to reproduce in his poetry not only the words—and in their limited range, too, actually used in common speech—but their sound.

"To carry this idea a little further it does not seem possible to me that a man can read on the printed page what he has never heard. Nobody today knows how to read Homer and Virgil perfectly, because the people who spoke Homer's Greek and Virgil's Latin are as dead as the sound of their language.

"On the other hand, to further emphasize the impossibility of words rather than sound conveying the sense of meaning, take the matter of translation. Really to understand and catch all that is embodied in a foreign masterpiece it must be read in the original, because while the words may be brought over, the tone cannot be.

"In the matter of poetry," the poet continued, "there is a subtle differentiation between sound and the sound of sense, which ought to be perfectly understood before I can make clear my position.

"For a second let me turn aside and say that the beginning of literary form is in some turn given to the sentence in folk speech. Art is the amplification and sophistication of the proverbial turns of speech.

"All folk speech is musical. In primitive conditions man has not at his aid reactions by which he can quickly and easily convey his ideas and emotions. Consequently, he has to think more deeply to call up the image for the communication of his meaning. It was the actuality he sought; and thinking more deeply, not in the speculative sense of science or scholarship, he carried out Carlyle's assertion that if you 'think deep enough you think musically.'

"Poetry has seized on this sound of speech and carried it to artificial and meaningless lengths. We have it exemplified in Sidney Lanier's musical notation of verse, where all the tones of the human voice in natural speech are entirely eliminated, leaving the sound of sense without root in experience."

CONVERSATIONS ON THE CRAFT
OF POETRY

*When Holt, Rinehart & Winston published the third edition of
Cleanth Brooks' and Robert Penn Warren's* Understanding Poetry *in
1959, they issued with it a tape supplement called "Conversations on
the Craft of Poetry." The tape was a discussion on technique and
practical craftsmanship, and had four participants: Brooks, Warren,
Frost, and Holt editor Kenney Withers. Frost, however, is obviously
the star performer; happily, Brooks and Warren are content to act as
catalysts to his ideas.*

WITHERS: Mr. Frost, I once heard you say that for a poem to
stick it must have a dramatic accent.

FROST: If it doesn't, it will not stay in anybody's head. It won't
be *catchy*. [. . .]
Catchiness has a lot to do with it, all of it, all the way up from
the ballads you hear on the street to the lines in Shakespeare that
stay with you without your trying to remember them. I just say
catchy. They stick on you like burrs thrown on you in holiday
foolery. You don't have to try to remember them. It's from the
way they're said, you know, an archness or something.

WARREN: Well, I'm sure you're right about the dramatic quality
being the basic quality of good poetry. That would bring up the
relation of meter and rhythm to the dramatic moment—moment by
moment—in a poem, wouldn't it?

FROST: That's right.

WARREN: I'd like to hear you say it in your way, how meter
enters into this picture—the dramatic quality.

FROST: The meter seems to be the basis of—the waves and the
beat of the heart seems to be basic in all making of poetry in all
languages—some sort of meter.

WARREN: The strain of the rhythm against the meter. Is that itself
just a dramatic fact that permeates a poem?

FROST: From those two things rises what we call this tune that's different from the tune of the other kind of music. It's a music of itself. And when people say that this will easily turn into—be set to music, I think it's bad writing. It ought to fight being set to music if it's got expression in it.

BROOKS: Yes, there's something resistant and unique in it; you can't just turn it into something else. This is to overstate the matter, but I do want to get it clear, if I can for myself: Would you say that even though the meter is based on the human pulse or some kind of basic rhythm in our natures, still for the poet it's something to be played over against—it's something to be fought with, to be tussled with? It's not directly expressive—ta-DA, ta-DA, ta-DA, ta-DA, ta-DA.

FROST: No, it's doggerel when you do that. You see, and how you save it from doggerel is having enough dramatic meaning in it for the other thing to break the doggerel. And it mustn't break *with* it.

I said years ago that it reminds me of a donkey and a donkey cart; for some of the time the cart is on the tugs and some of the time on the hold-backs. You see it's that way all the time. The one's doing that and the other—the one's holding the thing back and the other's pushing it forward—and so on, back and forward. . . . I puzzled over it many years and tried to make people see what I meant. They use the word "rhythm" about a lot of free verse; and gee, what's the good of the rhythm unless it is on something that trips it—that it ruffles? You know, it's got to ruffle the meter.

BROOKS: Isn't this the fault of—to name the name of a man who did write some very fine poems, I think: Vachel Lindsay depends too much on just the doggerel—the stamp of the . . .

FROST: Singsong, yes. And you know when he had something else, he thought he ought to put a note about it in the margin. Did you notice that?

BROOKS: Yes, to tell you how to read it.

FROST: "Say this in a golden tone," he says. You ought not to have to say that in the margin.

BROOKS: No, no. It's built in.

FROST: That ought to be in the meaning. This is why you have to have a meaning, 'cause you don't know what to do with anything if you don't have a meaning. It makes you act up; you've got to act up.

"What sayest thou, old barrelful of lies?" Chaucer says. What d'you say, "old barrelful of lies"? And you can hear it talk just the same today—and all of it. That's why it exists. It's beautiful, anywhere you look into Chaucer:

> Since I from love escaped am so fat,
> I never think to have been in his prison lean;
> Since I am free, I count him not a bean.

This is Chaucer talking too. It's just the same now. I hear the country people talking, England and here, with these same ways of acting up. Put it that way—call it "acting up."

You act up when you talk. Some do more than others. Some little children do: some just seem to be rather straight line, but some switch their whole body when they talk—switch their skirts. *Expressiveness* comes over them. Words aren't enough.

And of course all before words came the expressiveness—groans and murmurs and things like that emerging into words. And some few of these linger, like "um-hnm" and "unh-unh" and "mmm" and all our groans. By myself sometimes I groan at something already done that I'd like to avert.

WARREN: From a groan to a sonnet's a straight line.

FROST: Yes, that's right.

WARREN: You are distinguishing, then, the meaning in the most limited sense from the over-all, felt meaning of the whole thing. Is that it?

FROST: That's your whole guide, the over-all meaning.

WARREN: That's your guide and your end product.

FROST: Yes, your end product. And also, you know, one of the funny things is that this *mood* you're writing in foretells the end product. See, it begins sort of that way and a way of talking that foretells the end product. There's a logic of that sort of thing.

Somebody said to be a master writer you don't have to wait for your moods. That'd be like Browning as he got older. You get to be a virtuoso, and you aren't a poet any more. He'd lost his moods somewhere. He'd got to be a master. We don't want to be masters.

WARREN: In other words you don't want even to be master—is that right?—of the particular poem. Before you start you're moving from mood to the exploration of the mood, is that it?

BROOKS: Poem is a discovery. . . .

FROST: Yes, that's right. You're on a little voyage of discovery. And there's a logic in it. You're going to come out somewhere with great certainty. And you can tell whether you've lost it on the way. And you throw the poem away—if you lose it.

WARREN: Yes.

FROST: Down the years, looking back over it all. And you see, a good many who think they're writing free verse are really writing old-fashioned iambic. A good deal of Whitman's like that, and a lot of Masters is like that: he just never got away from blank verse—the sound of blank verse.

And so there are places where this thing takes place that I'm talking about—there's both the meter and the expressiveness on it—and so we get a poem.

Ezra Pound used to say that you've got to get all the meter out of it—extirpate the meter. If you do, maybe you've got true free verse, and I don't want any of it!

WARREN: Well, you can go at it another way: I guess it's Winters who said that behind all good free verse—I may be misinterpreting him, but I think that's what he says—behind all good free verse there's a shadow of formal verse.

FROST: That's right. And if we hadn't had the years of formal verse, this stuff wouldn't be any good, you know. The shadow is there; that's what gives it any charm it has. You see, I'm hard on free verse a little—too hard, I know.

BROOKS: Would you be hard, Mr. Frost, also, on the business of the beatniks and chanting poetry to jazz? Is that letting too much of music—of the wrong side of music come in?

FROST: Yes, absolutely. Death! Hang 'em all!

This fellow that's going to talk with me (A. P. Herbert from London) tomorrow, they've told me what his prejudices are, you know, to see if they couldn't rouse me to say something to him. He's in favor of hanging delinquent children. That's the funniest prejudice. And he'd be in favor of exterminating the free-verse writers, I'm pretty sure. I'm not as bad as that.

Let's put it this way, that prose and verse are alike in having high poetic possibilities of ideas, and free verse is anywhere you want to be between those two things, prose and verse. I like to say, guardedly, that I could define poetry this way: It is that which is lost out of both prose and verse in translation. That means something in the way the words are curved and all that—the way the words are taken, the way you take the words.

WARREN: The best-order notion: the old Coleridgean best-order notion.

FROST: Yes, I'm pretty extreme about it.

You know, I've given offense by saying that I'd as soon write free verse as play tennis with the net down. I want something there—the other thing—something to hold and something for me to put a strain on; and I'd be lost in the air with just cutting loose —unless I'm in my other mood of making it prose right out, you know, and I don't write much of that. But that's another thing. [. . .]

BROOKS: Speaking of tune, Yeats said that he started a poem with a little tune in his head.

FROST: Yeats said a good many things, and I've talked with him about that. He said that nothing he hated more than having his poems set to music. It stole the show. It wasn't the tune he heard in his ear. And what this other thing is. . . . If he meant a tune, it doesn't seem to go with that, does it?

Burns without any doubt had old music—old songs—in his head that he wrote from. But I don't think that of Yeats; I don't know what he meant by that. But if he meant a tune. . . . I have a tune, but it's a tune of the blend of these two things. Something rises— it's neither one of these things. It's neither the meter nor the rhythm; it's a tune arising from the stress on those—same as your fingers on the strings, you know. The twang!

WARREN: The twang.

FROST: The twang of one on the other. And I don't know what he meant. I think he must have meant what we mean: from a result of something beginning to rise from it right away when you're playing one on the other; that's what he carried. There must be a oneness as you're doing it. You aren't putting two things together —laying them together. It isn't synthetic like that; no.

BROOKS: No, it's growing a plant, not building a wall.

WARREN: Growing in terms of this dominating mood—is that right?—that you referred to as a germ of the poem?

FROST: Yes.

WARREN: The tune is the mood groping for its logic, is that it? Something like that?

FROST: That's right; that's right, yes. I'm glad that we feel that way together. Yes, you know that, when I begin a poem I don't know—I don't want a poem that I can tell was written toward a good ending—one sentence, you know. That's trickery. You've got to be the happy discoverer of your ends.

BROOKS: That's a very fine way of phrasing it, "the happy discoverer of your end." Because otherwise it is contrived. You can see it coming a mile off.

FROST: A mile away.

I've often said that another definition of poetry is dawn—that it's something dawning on you while you're writing it. It comes off if it really dawns when the light comes at the end. And the feeling of dawn—the freshness of dawn—that you didn't think this all out and write it in prose first and then translate it into verse. That's abhorrent! [. . .]

One of the things that I notice with myself is that I can't make certain word sounds go together, sometimes; they won't say. This has got something to do with the way one vowel runs into another, the way one syllable runs into another. And then I never know—I don't like to reason about that too much. I don't understand it, but I've changed lines because there was something about them that my ear refused. And I suppose it has something to do with this vowels and consonants.

You know what I've thought sometimes: that the mouth and throat are like this, that it's certain sounds are here, and you can't go right from this one to that one; you've got to go like this. The mouth's got to be doing that inside. I don't know.

But gee, you know, I don't want any science of it. It's got to be—not trial and error. You don't correct it if you're going well—if you're felicitous—if you're having a happy day.

Well, we've come a good way. And it's fun. I don't often sit

with somebody to talk about it this way. Sometimes from the plat-
form I say some of these things, you know. And I used to do it
more than I do it now. I had a notion I had to tell the public how
to read lines. Then I decided no; that's in them anyway. They all
had Mother Goose and everything. Don't you see that you throw
them back on their Mother Goose? And then all with the play of
ideas in it; how deep the Mother Goose is, you see:

> Pussy cat, pussy cat, where have you been?
> I've been to London to see the Coronation!

To pervert a little:

> Pussy cat, pussy cat, what did you see there?
> I saw nothing but what I might have seen just
>   as well by staying right here in Nashville!
> I saw a mouse run under a chair.

And that's very deep. But it's so pretty the way it's set off, you
know, and nobody need see it at all unless they're any discerning.
"I saw a mouse run under a chair." That's meant a lot to me, that
has, all my life.

WARREN: That's a good one.

FROST: That's what makes regionalists, you see. You could stay
right at home and see it all.

You know another thing I think belongs to poetry is fresh observation, don't you? All the time, little insights. They say "nothing new," but there is all the time. For instance, I was saying about
women the other day—they were plaguing me to leave some boys
I wanted to talk to; they thought I was getting tired or something.
Finally I turned on them, and I said, "A woman would rather take
care of you than listen to you think."

WARREN: That's a mark of a good woman.

FROST: And then I softened that to them by saying, "That's why
we like you, my dears. You see, because we know that what we
think doesn't amount to much anyway, we men." You see, that
was a fresh observation.

WARREN: Well, the mere observation of just the facts of the world is a constant refresher for poetry. It's a waking up of yourself when you get the least little turn of an observation of the way a leaf or a light is, or something.

FROST: Little insights into a character and a little observation of something growing. You know how it does, something with life. [. . .]

Parodies

A PARODY OF THE CELTIC DRAMA

Frost wrote this parody as a joke. One of his friends, James Wells, owned a small private printing press and asked Frost for a manuscript to print. Frost gave him this parody of the Celtic drama, which had indeed been getting "smaller and smaller" under the influence of the Japanese Noh plays. Wells extended the literary joke by printing it in a separate volume with an elaborately pretentious format.

THE COW'S IN THE CORN

This, my sole contribution to the Celtic Drama (no one so unromantic as not to have made at least one) illustrates the latter day tendency of all drama to become smaller and smaller and to be acted in smaller and smaller theatres to smaller and smaller audiences.

R.F.

A kitchen. Afternoon. Through all O'Toole
Behind an open paper reads Home Rule.
His wife irons clothes. She bears the family load.
A shout is heard from someone on the road.

Mrs. O'Toole.

Johnny, hear that? The cow is in the corn!

Mr. O'Toole.

I hear you say it.

Mrs. O'Toole.

Well then if you do
Why don't you go and drive her in the barn?

Mr. O'Toole.

I'm waiting; give me time.

164

Mrs. O'Toole.

Waiting, says you!
Waiting for what, God keep you always poor!
The cow is in the corn, I say again.

Mr. O'Toole.

Whose corn's she in?

Mrs. O'Toole.

Our own, you may be sure.

Mr. O'Toole.

Go drive her into someone else's then!

She lifts her flat iron at him. To escape her
He slightly elevates the open paper.
The cow's heard mooing through the window (right).
For curtain let the scene stay on till night.

VERS-LIBRE PARODY OF EZRA POUND

This parody-attack on Ezra Pound was enclosed in a letter that Frost sent to F. S. Flint. (Compare page 87) It was never sent to Pound.

[*c.* 20 July 1913] [Beaconsfield]

I am a Mede and Persian
In my acceptance of harsh laws laid down for me
When you said I could not read
When you said I looked old
When you said I was slow of wit
I knew that you only meant
That you could read

That you looked young
That you were nimble of wit
But I took your words at their face value
I accepted your words like an encyclical letter
It did not matter
At worst they were good medicine
I made my stand elsewhere
I did not ask you to unsay them.
I was willing to take anything you said from you
If I might be permitted to hug the illusion
That you liked my poetry
And liked it for the right reason.

You reviewed me,
And I was not sure—
I was afraid it was not artis[ti]cally done.
I decided I couldnt use it to impress my friends
Much less my enemies.
But in as much [as] it was praise I was grateful
For praise I do love.

I suspected though that in praising me
You were not concerned so much with my desert
As with your power
That you praised me arbitrarily
And took credit to yourself
In demonstrating that you could thrust anything
          upon the world
Were it never so humble
And bid your will avouch it

And here we come close to what I demanded of you
     I did not want the money that you were disbursing
     among your favorites
     for two American editors.
                              Not that.
All I asked was that you should hold to one thing
That you considered me a poet.

That was [why] I clung to you
　　As one clings to a group of insincere friends
　　For fear they shall turn their thoughts against him
　　　　the moment he is out of hearing.
The truth is I was afraid of you

A PARODY OF VACHEL LINDSAY

Untermeyer explains the background to this parody when he publishes it in The Letters of Robert Frost to Louis Untermeyer. *Vachel Lindsay once suggested to Sara Teasdale, Frost, and Untermeyer that they all write a poem on the same subject and publish the poems together. The subject he suggested was heavyweight champion John L. Sullivan, whom he saw rather idealistically as the pugnacious spirit of frontier Americanism. No one appears to have thought anything more of the idea until Frost enclosed his contribution in a letter to Untermeyer.*

JOHN L. SULLIVAN ENTERS HEAVEN
(To be sung to the tune of "Heaven Overarches You and Me")

Sullivan arrived at the very lowest Heaven
Which is sometimes mistaken for the very highest Hell,
Where barkeeps, pugilists, jockeys, and gamblers
And the women corresponding (if there are any) dwell.
　　They done queer things, but they done 'em on the level,
　　And thus they escape the jurisdiction of the Devil.

Sullivan felt, and he couldn't find his ticket.
He thought for a moment he would have to go to Hell.
But the gatekeeper told him, "You don't need a ticket:
Everybody knows you: Your name's John L.
　　There's a lot of fighting characters been setting up waiting
　　To see if you were up to your mundane rating."

Sullivan asked, "They've been setting up to see me?"
And the gatekeeper answered, "They have like Hell!
They've been setting up to try you, and see if they can lick you,
And settle who's who in the Fields of Asphodel.
    So you may as well be ready to take them all on—
    Hercules and Pollux and the whole doggone.

"Fraternity of sluggers, I mean the first-raters
(We send the second-raters to entertain Hell).
I seen Herc's hands all wound with lead and leather
Till they looked like the balls on a great dumb-bell.
    He's mad because the deeds you matched his with
    Were sound printed facts, while his were just myth."

Sullivan said "I guess I'm in for trouble."
He cracked the gate a little and then said "Hell!
I hope I ain't expected to take all them together.
If I take them in succession I'll be doing damn well.
    I wish I'd staid in Boston or Chelsea, and would of
    If I'd had the least encouragement to think I could of."

The gatekeeper said "You don't need to worry;
The way to do's to rush them and give them sudden Hell.
They've been so purged of earthliness they don't weigh nothing
While *you* weigh something, and will for a spell.
    They've nothing to sustain them but their jealousy of you,
    While you still feel the good of Boston beans, you do."

Sullivan burst into Heaven roaring.
The devils beyond the board fences of Hell
Put the whites of their eyes to crannies and knotholes
To see who was driving the angels pell-mell.
    They said 'twas the greatest punch of all times.
    Ring the bells of Heaven! Sound the gladsome chimes!

                                                        R.F.

    This can only be read successfully by the author. You can read
it yourself from the book for the price of the book: one dollar.
You can hear the author read it for one hundred dollars. It is worth
the difference.

Marginalia

FROST'S COMMENTS ON POUND

These marginal comments occur in the presentation copy of Ripostes which Pound gave to Frost, and which is now in the Special Collections Library of New York University. They were undoubtedly an answer to Pound's attempts to do for Frost what he did for Eliot; Frost refused to consider Pound as "il miglior fabbro." The comments seem to have no single aim: they are partly simple explanations (e.g., l. 8), partly a parody of Pound's own critical blue-pencilling in his desperate concern to make everything shorter (l. 1), and partly Frost's own irritated judgments (l. 18). Line numbers have been added to the text below, and the marginal comments are given at the end.

PORTRAIT D'UNE FEMME

Your mind and you are our Sargasso Sea,   1
London has swept about you this score years
And bright ships left you this or that in fee:
Ideas, old gossip, oddments of all things,
Strange spars of knowledge and dimmed wares of price.   5
Great minds have sought you—lacking someone else.
You have been second always. Tragical?
No. You preferred it to the usual thing:
One dull man, dulling and uxorious,
One average mind—with one thought less, each year.   10
Oh, you are patient, I have seen you sit
Hours, where something might have floated up.
And now you pay one. Yes, you richly pay.
You are a person of some interest, one comes to you
And takes strange gain away: 15
Trophies fished up; some curious suggestion;
Fact that leads nowhere; and a tale for two,
Pregnant with mandrakes, or with something else
That might prove useful and yet never proves,
That never fits a corner or shows use,   20

Or finds its hour upon the loom of days:
The tarnished, gaudy, wonderful old work;
Idols and ambergris and rare inlays,
These are your riches, your great store; and yet
For all this sea-hoard of deciduous things,   25
Strange woods half sodden, and new brighter stuff:
In the slow float of differing light and deep,
No! there is nothing! In the whole and all,
Nothing that's quite your own.
                    Yet this is you.   30

l. 1   "and you" crossed out, and "is" written above "are."

l. 2   "this score years" enclosed in parenthesis.

l. 3   "in fee" crossed out.

l. 5   "spars of knowledge" and "wares of price" both enclosed in parenthesis.

l. 8   after colon, Frost has written "viz, being somebodys stenographer."

l. 9   "Polyandry" is written in the margin before this line.

l. 12   "up" underlined and "in" written in the margin.

l. 14   above "some interest" is written "style:" and an arrow directing attention across the page to l. 27. "Some interest" is underlined.

l. 16   "Trophies" underlined and "Pledges" written in the margin.

l. 17   "for two" underlined and "Why" written in the margin.

l. 18   "Pregnant with mandrakes" underlined and "Bosh" written in the margin.

l. 20   "shows use" underlined and "Idiom: wear" written in the margin.

l. 21   downward strokes at each end of this line and "Nothing!" written in the margin.

l. 23   "ambergris" underlined and "Work?" written in the margin.

l. 26   a large cross-mark drawn in front of this line and "Balance without balance" written beside it.

l. 27   end of the arrow drawn from l. 14 at the beginning of this line; "deep" is underlined and "Miltonic" written in the margin.

l. 28   "and all" crossed out.

NOTE ON THE TEXTS

Part of the reason for the selection of these texts is the desire to demonstrate the range of literary forms in which Frost's criticism occurs. The only critical medium that has been excluded is conversation; for though Frost was a great conversationalist according to those who knew him well, he has, so far, lacked an adequate Boswell. The two books that purport to record his conversations— Louis Mertins' *Robert Frost: Life and Talks-Walking* and Daniel Smythe's *Robert Frost Speaks*—shows signs of Boswell's hero worship but not of his accuracy. The cadences they record are not always Frost's.

There are three published editions of Frost's letters: Louis Untermeyer's *Letters of Robert Frost to Louis Untermeyer*, Margaret [Bartlett] Anderson's *Robert Frost and John Bartlett: The Record of a Friendship*, and Lawrance Thompson's *Selected Letters of Robert Frost*. Fifteen of the letters in the preceding texts are taken from these volumes. Fourteen others have never been published. For these I am grateful to the following: The University of Texas for the F. S. Flint and John Freeman letters; Pennsylvania State University for the Amy Bonner letters; Columbia University for the John Erskine letters; The Library of Congress for the Lewis N. Chase letters; Plymouth State College for the George Browne letter; Dartmouth College for the Kimball Flaccus letter; and Harvard University for the Witter Bynner letter.

Of the four prefaces used, two have recently been collected by Hyde Cox and Edward Connery Lathem in their valuable edition *Selected Prose of Robert Frost*. "The Figure a Poem Makes" was the preface to the *Collected Poems* published in 1949. The delightful preface to the Dartmouth poetry anthology has not been republished since it appeared in 1925.

The two reviews have also been collected in the above *Selected Prose* volume; Frost used "The Prerequisites" as the preface to his collection *Aforesaid* in 1954.

Perhaps the aspect of his work that has received the least attention is his lectures. Of the hundreds of lectures Frost gave during his lifetime, hardly any have been published, though a volume of them is projected. These, presumably, would be the largest single source of Frost's critical opinions. But part of the difficulty in examining this medium is Frost's own recalcitrance. He never wrote out his lectures; he "lost" the series he was under contract to submit in writing to Harvard. Fortunately, many of the later ones are on tape and hence authentic, but in his early years of lecturing much of their value for us depends upon the notetaker. The two lectures selected for inclusion here, although they illustrate Frost's capacity as a lecturer, bring up the question of reliability of such second-hand presentation. The first—only recently discovered and now held by the Library of Plymouth State College, New Hampshire—was transcribed by George Browne from a series of lectures that Frost gave at the Browne and Nichols School in 1915, and seems to come close to Frost's way of thinking and talking. At any rate, when it was submitted to him for examination, Frost approved this transcription, and Browne incorporated part of it into an article for *The Independent* published on May 22, 1916, under the title "Robert Frost, A Poet of Speech." The second, also reported by Browne, did not have this official ratification, though the vocabulary is unmistakably Frost's. It too is held by Plymouth State College.

The two interviews, from the early and the late days of Frost's career, have been collected in a slightly shortened form in Edward Connery Lathem's *Interviews with Robert Frost*. Neither is wholly Frost at second hand, as interviews often tend to be. The discussion with Brooks and Warren was taped as a supplement to their *Understanding Poetry*. The Braithwaite interview was based largely on material that Frost was careful to supply him with in a letter that Lawrance Thompson publishes in *Selected Letters of Robert Frost* (Letter 105).

Parodies may seem to be criticism-via-the-back-door. Yet they do indicate a literary attitude, if not always a definite judgment. "The Cow's in the Corn" is a light jibe at the renascent Celtic drama, written in 1929 for a friend, James Wells, who had a dilettante interest in private publishing and owned the Slide Mountain

Press. This "play" came out in a separate volume, ornately printed in an elaborate format. The parody on Vachel Lindsay's "General William Booth Enters Heaven" hits its mark less surely, partly because it is longer, and partly because it ignores the musical notation that was the central feature of Lindsay's poem; but it does indicate Frost's contempt for Lindsay's misguidedness. The free-verse "letter" to Ezra Pound is only half parody, though it does catch the totally irregular rhythms and line lengths of *vers-libre;* its attitude toward Pound is serious, bitter, sensitive to the difference in their temperaments and aims. Frost in fact never sent it to Pound. He sent it instead to F. S. Flint, who advised him against an open break with Pound; and Frost stood by this advice.

The poetic and temperamental clashes with Pound are again evident in the notes that Frost wrote in the margins of "Portrait D'une Femme," in his copy of *Ripostes*. This volume is part of Frost's personal library that Mrs. Lesley Frost Ballantine recently donated to the Special Collections Library of New York University. Frost's blue-penciling of "Portrait" was clearly an irritated answer to Pound's attempts to shorten and correct "infelicities" in Frost's poems, but he was also clearly ill at ease with the subject, the technique, and some of the imagery. Note his "Bosh" beside the phrase "pregnant with mandrakes."

The texts are not presented in chronological order. They are arranged in sections according to their literary forms, and, within each form, according to Frost's development of ideas and interests. Cross reference to the texts is indicated by the rubric (Page —) in the body of the introductory analysis.

Frost's spelling and punctuation are sometimes erratic. They are presented as they occur in the original manuscript, without the distracting use of *sic*, and uncorrected unless correction is necessary for intelligibility. Such corrections are noted in brackets.

Ellipses are indicated by the following notation: three dots whenever part of a sentence is omitted; four dots whenever a full sentence or more is omitted; and three dots enclosed in brackets whenever a full paragraph or more is omitted.

Notes

THE SCOPE OF FROST'S CRITICISM

1. Robert Frost, "The Prerequisites," *Selected Prose of Robert Frost,* ed. Hyde Cox and Edward Connery Lathem (New York: Holt, Rinehart & Winston, 1966), p. 97.

2. T. S. Eliot, "Tradition and the Individual Talent," *Selected Prose,* ed. John Hayward (Harmondsworth: Penguin, 1953), p. 23.

3. Lawrance Thompson (ed.), *Selected Letters of Robert Frost* (New York: Holt, Rinehart & Winston, 1964), p. 385.

4. Eliot, "Tradition and the Individual Talent," p. 30.

5. Ezra Pound, "A Retrospect," *Literary Essays of Ezra Pound,* ed. T. S. Eliot (New York: New Directions Paperback, 1968).

6. W. B. Yeats, "The Municipal Gallery Revisited," *Collected Poems* (London: Macmillan, 1955), p. 369.

7. Thompson, *Selected Letters,* p. 79.

8. *Ibid.,* 343.

9. Louis Mertins, *Robert Frost: Life and Talks-Walking* (Norman, Okla.: University of Oklahoma Press, 1965), p. 372.

10. *Ibid.,* 372.

11. *Ibid.,* 304.

12. Thompson, *Selected Letters,* p. 557.

13. Robert Frost, "Education by Poetry," *Selected Prose,* p. 35.

14. Mertins, *Life and Talks-Walking,* p. 251.

15. Lawrance Thompson, *Robert Frost: The Early Years* (New York: Holt, Rinehart & Winston, 1966), pp. 504–505.

16. Unpublished letter from Robert Frost to Lewis Gannett, February 3, 1927 (Special Collections Library, Columbia University).

17. Unpublished letter from Robert Frost to Ashley Thorndike, January 25, 1916 (Special Collections Library, Columbia University).

18. Unpublished letter from Robert Frost to Norman Foerster, October 25, 1931 (Special Collections Library, Stanford University).

19. Thompson, *Selected Letters,* p. 425.

FROST AS A CRITICAL THEORIST

1. Louis Untermeyer (ed.), *The Letters of Robert Frost to Louis Untermeyer* (New York: Holt, Rinehart & Winston, 1963), p. 16.

2. See Frost's recognition of this in "The Craft of Poetry," *Interviews with Robert Frost*, ed. Edward Connery Lathem (New York: Holt, Rinehart & Winston, 1966), p. 203.

3. Edgar Allan Poe, "The Rationale of Verse," *The Complete Works of Edgar Allan Poe*. Vol. 14. (The Monticello edition; New York: George D. Sproul, 1902), p. 220.

4. Unpublished transcript by Amy Bonner of a lecture given by Robert Frost at the New School for Social Research, N.Y., in 1937. (Special Collections Library, Pennsylvania State University.)

5. Thompson, *Selected Letters*, p. 25.

6. Newspaper interview, quoted in Robert Newdick, "Robert Frost and the Sound of Sense," *American Literature*, IX (November, 1937), p. 298.

7. Sidney Cox, *A Swinger of Birches* (New York: New York University Press, 1957), p. 11.

8. J. M. Synge, Preface to *The Playboy of the Western World*, *The Complete Works of John M. Synge* (New York: Random House, 1935), p. 4.

9. Robert Frost, "A Visit in Franconia," *Interviews with Robert Frost*, p. 13.

10. Cox, *A Swinger of Birches*, p. 110.

11. Thompson, *Selected Letters*, p. 130.

12. *Ibid.*, 217.

13. *Ibid.*, 151.

14. The American Dramatic Society produced "The Death of the Hired Man" and "Home Burial" in 1915; the Breadloaf Writers Conference staged "Snow" in 1925.

15. Robert Frost, "Preface to *A Way Out*," *Selected Prose*, p. 13.

16. Thompson, *Selected Letters*, p. 182.

17. Untermeyer, *Letters*, p. 10.

18. Unpublished postcard from Robert Frost to F. S. Flint, n.d. (The Academic Center Library, University of Texas).

19. Thompson, *Selected Letters*, pp. 191–192.

20. See Paul Fussell, *Poetic Meter and Poetic Form* (New York: Random House, 1965), Chap. I.

21. Thompson, *Selected Letters*, p. 128.

22. *Ibid.*, 242.

23. *Ibid.*, 361.

24. *Ibid.*, 179.

25. *Ibid.*, 465.

26. *Ibid.*, 369.

27. Robert Frost, *The Poetry of Robert Frost*, ed. Edward Connery Lathem (New York: Holt, Rinehart & Winston, 1969), p. 484.

28. Untermeyer, *Letters*, p. 14.

29. *Ibid.*, 17.

30. *Ibid.*, 230.

31. Thompson, *Selected Letters*, p. 344.

32. Robert Frost, "Education by Poetry," *Selected Prose*, pp. 44–45.

33. Untermeyer, *Letters*, p. 22.

34. Lawrance Thompson, *Fire and Ice: The Art and Thought of Robert Frost* (New York: Holt, Rinehart and Winston, 1942), Chap. 2.

35. Thompson, *Selected Letters*, p. 237.

36. Untermeyer, *Letters*, p. 256.

37. Thompson, *Selected Letters*, pp. 324–325.

38. *Ibid.*, 61.

39. Untermeyer, *Letters*, pp. 75–76.

40. Richard Poirier, "Robert Frost," *Paris Review*, No. 24 (Summer-Fall, 1959), p. 115.

41. Frost, "Education by Poetry," *Selected Prose*, p. 36.

42. *Ibid.*, 37.

43. *Ibid.*, 41.

FROST AS A PRACTICAL CRITIC

1. Thompson, *Selected Letters*, p. 385.

2. Mertins, *Life and Talks-Walking*, p. 197.

3. Thompson, *Selected Letters*, p. 21.

4. *Ibid.*, 83.

5. Unpublished letter from Robert Frost to Mark Van Doren, December 1, 1935 (Special Collections Library, Columbia University).

6. Thompson, *Selected Letters*, pp. 103–104.

7. *Ibid.*, 151.

8. *Ibid.*, 142.

9. This book is in the Special Collections Library, New York University.

10. Untermeyer, *Letters*, p. 75.

11. *Ibid.*, 17.

12. Poirier, *Paris Review* interview, p. 99.

13. Mertins, *Life and Talks-Walking*, p. 353.

14. Elizabeth Shepley Sergeant, *Robert Frost: The Trial by Existence* (New York: Holt, Rinehart & Winston, 1960), p. 363.

15. Unpublished letter from Robert Frost to John Erskine, January 18, 1923 (Special Collections Library, Columbia University).

16. Thompson, *Selected Letters*, p. 179. There are seven poems by Lawrance in the anthology to which Frost was referring—*Some Imagiste Poems: An Anthology* (Boston: Houghton Mifflin Co., 1915). They are: "Ballad of Another Ophelia," "Illicit," "Fireflies in the Corn," "A Woman and her Dead Husband," "The Mowers," "Scent of Irises," and "Green."

17. *Ibid.*, 139.

18. Unpublished letter from Robert Frost to John Erskine, n.d. (Special Collections Library, Columbia University).

19. Untermeyer, *Letters*, pp. 175–176.

20. Thompson, *Selected Letters*, p. 369.

21. *Ibid.*, 217.

22. *Ibid.*, 306.

23. Untermeyer, *Letters*, p. 255.

24. Poirier, *Paris Review* interview, p. 109.

25. Ben Miller sent a copy of this letter to Mark Van Doren. The copy is now in the Special Collections Library, Columbia University.

26. Thompson, *Selected Letters*, p. 219.

27. Untermeyer, *Letters*, pp. 62–63.

28. *Ibid.*, 106–107.

29. *Ibid.*, 174.

30. Thompson, *Selected Letters*, p. 291.

31. Robert Frost, "Robert Frost, New American Poet," *Interviews*, p. 7.

32. Frost's personal library—at least what it contained at the time of his death—is now in the Special Collections Library, New York University.

33. Thompson, *Selected Letters*, p. 265.

34. *Ibid.*, 554.

35. Quoted by Untermeyer, *Letters*, p. 130.

36. *Ibid.*, 203.

37. Mertins, *Life and Talks-Walking*, p. 385.

38. In the Special Collections Library, New York University.

39. Thompson, Lawrance, *Robert Frost: The Early Years, 1874–1915* (New York: Holt, Rinehart & Winston, 1966), p. 549.

40. Thompson, *Selected Letters*, p. 182.

41. See, for example, the excellent study by Reuben Brower, *The Poetry of Robert Frost: Constellations of Intention* (New York: Oxford University Press, 1963), Chap. 3.

Bibliography

BIBLIOGRAPHIES

American Literary Manuscripts. Compiled and published under the auspices of the American Literature Group, Modern Language Association of America, by the Committee on Manuscript Holdings. Austin: University of Texas Press, 1960.

Clymer, W. B. Shubrick, and Green, Charles R. *Robert Frost: A Bibliography*. Amherst: The Jones Library, 1937.

Hamer, Philip May (ed.). *A Guide to Archives and Manuscripts in the United States*. New Haven: Yale University Press, 1961.

Mertins, Louis and Esther. *The Intervals of Robert Frost: A Critical Bibliography*. Berkeley: University of California Press, 1947.

The National Union Catalogue of Manuscript Collections. Compiled and edited, annually since 1959, by the Manuscripts Section of the Descriptive Cataloguing Division of the Library of Congress.

PRIMARY MATERIAL

Anderson, Margaret (Bartlett). *Robert Frost and John Bartlett: The Record of a Friendship*. New York: Holt, Rinehart & Winston, 1963.

Cox, Hyde, and Lathem, Edward Connery (eds.). *Selected Prose of Robert Frost*. New York: Holt, Rinehart & Winston, 1966.

Cox, Sidney. *A Swinger of Birches*. New York: New York University Press, 1957.

Lathem, Edward Connery (ed.). *Interviews with Robert Frost*. New York: Holt, Rinehart & Winston, 1966.

———— (ed.). *The Poetry of Robert Frost*. New York: Holt, Rinehart & Winston, 1969.

————, and Thompson, Lawrance (eds.). *Robert Frost and the Lawrence, Massachusetts, "High School Bulletin."* Facsimile edition. New York: The Grolier Club, 1966.

Mertins, Louis. *Robert Frost: Life and Talks-Walking*. Norman, Okla.: University of Oklahoma Press, 1965.

Munson, Gorham B. *Robert Frost: A Study in Sensibility and Good Sense*. New York: George H. Doran Co., 1927.

Reeve, F. D. *Robert Frost in Russia*. Boston: Little, Brown, 1963.

Sergeant, Elizabeth Shepley. *Robert Frost: The Trial by Existence*. New York: Holt, Rinehart & Winston, 1960.

Smythe, Daniel. *Robert Frost Speaks*. New York: Twayne, 1964.

Thompson, Lawrance (ed.). *Selected Letters of Robert Frost*. New York: Holt, Rinehart & Winston, 1964.

Untermeyer, Louis (ed.). *The Letters of Robert Frost to Louis Untermeyer*. New York: Holt, Rinehart & Winston, 1963.

SECONDARY MATERIAL

A. *Books*

Brower, Reuben. *The Poetry of Robert Frost: Constellations of Intention*. New York: Oxford University Press, 1963.

Ciardi, John (ed.). *Mid-Century American Poets*. New York: Twayne, 1950.

Coffin, Robert P. Tristram. *New Poets of New England: Frost and Robinson*. Baltimore: The Johns Hopkins Press, 1938.

Cox, James M. (ed.). *Robert Frost: A Collection of Critical Essays*. Englewood Cliffs, New Jersey: Prentice-Hall, 1966.

Elliott, G. R. *The Cycle of Modern Poetry*. Princeton: Princeton University Press, 1929.

Fussell, Paul Jr. *Poetic Meter and Poetic Form*. New York: Random House, 1965.

Gould, Jean. *Robert Frost: The Aim Was Song*. New York: Dodd, Mead, 1964.

Hoffman, Daniel G. (ed.). *American Poetry and Poetics*. New York: Doubleday, 1962.

Isaacs, Elizabeth. *An Introduction to Robert Frost*. Denver: Alan Swallow, 1962.

Lowell, Amy. *Tendencies in Modern American Poetry*. New York: Macmillan, 1917.

Marsh, Edward H. (ed.). *Georgian Poetry 1911–1912*. London: The Poetry Bookshop, 1913.

———. *Georgian Poetry 1913–1915*. New York: G. P. Putnam's Sons, 1916.

———. *Georgian Poetry 1916–1917*. London: The Poetry Bookshop, 1917.

Ransom, John Crowe. *The New Criticism*. Norfolk, Conn.: New Directions, 1941.

Richards, I. A. *Principles of Literary Criticism*. New York: Harcourt, Brace, 1930.

Squires, Radcliffe. *The Major Themes of Robert Frost*. Ann Arbor: University of Michigan Press, 1963.

Synge, John M. *The Complete Works of John M. Synge*. New York: Random House, 1935.

Thompson, Lawrance. *Fire and Ice: The Art and Thought of Robert Frost*. New York: Holt, Rinehart and Winston, 1942.

———. *Robert Frost: The Early Years, 1874–1915*. New York: Holt, Rinehart & Winston, 1966.

———. *Robert Frost: The Years of Triumph, 1915–1938*. New York: Holt, Rinehart & Winston, 1970.

Thornton, Richard (ed.). *Recognition of Robert Frost*. New York: Henry Holt & Co., 1937.

Yeats, W. B. *Collected Poems*. London: Macmillan, 1955.

B. *Articles and Essays*

Carlson, Eric W. "Robert Frost on 'Vocal Imagination': the Merger of Form and Content," *American Literature*, XXXIII (January, 1962), 519–522.

Ciardi, John. "Robert Frost: The Way to the Poem," *The Saturday Review*, XLI (April 12, 1958), 13–15, 65.

Cook, Reginald C. "Frost on Analytical Criticism," *College English*, XVII (May, 1956), 434–438.

Cox, Sidney. "The Courage to be New: A Reappraisal of Robert Frost," *Vermont History*, XXII (April, 1954), 119–126.

Emerson, Ralph Waldo. "The Poet," *The Complete Works of Ralph Waldo Emerson*. Vol. III. Century edition. Boston: Houghton, Mifflin, 1903.

Mulder, William. "Freedom and Form: Robert Frost's Double Discipline," *South Atlantic Quarterly*, LIV (July, 1955), 386–393.

Newdick, Robert S. "Robert Frost and the Sound of Sense," *American Literature*, IX (November, 1937), 289–300.

———. "Robert Frost and the Dramatic," *New England Quarterly*, X (June, 1937), 263–269.

———. "Robert Frost's Other Harmony," *Sewanee Review*, XLVIII (July–September, 1940), 409–418.

Poe, Edgar Allan, "The Rationale of Verse," *The Complete Works of Edgar Allan Poe*. Vol. 14. The Monticello edition. New York: George D. Sproul, 1902.

Poirier, Richard. "Robert Frost," *Paris Review*, No. 24 (Summer–Fall, 1959), 89–120.

Winters, Yvor. "Robert Frost, or The Spiritual Drifter as Poet," *Sewanee Review*, LVI (Autumn, 1948), 564–596.